What readers are saying about Kidd and Spitfire Doll

Don't miss this book! You will love these people and the fantastic true story of their lives and miracles! Very good writing. I highly recommend it. I loved it and never wanted to put it down.

Letha H.

I read Kidd in a 24 hour period. It's rather obvious that I was not bored at any time! I think the publication is great with the details of Yates and Dollie in early life and the unique way God brought them together. I give you an A+ ! You are a gifted writer! *Dr. Bill Sheeks*

Kidd and Spitfire Doll is a page turner that you are going to enjoy reading. Jonnie is a wonderful person and writes extremely well!

Marietta S.

I loved your book; wonderful writing. My wife and I read it in two days because we couldn't put it down. It was so good we passed it around!

M. A. P.

When I start a book I lose interest and never finish. Kidd and Spitfire Doll is the first book I have ever finished and I didn't want it to end. I loved it so much and I can't wait to read the next one.

Dianna B.

Kidd and Spitfire Doll is like a breath of fresh air! A wonderful book, it depicts the Pentecostal life in such a way that will touch many hearts for Christ. -

Patricia T.

Just finished Kidd and Spitfire Doll. Well done, Jonnie. I love it and can't wait to read part two! *Lesa H.*

I just finished your book and I had to tell you how much I enjoyed it! Thank you for sharing such a wonderful testimony. I thoroughly enjoyed reading it and I look forward to the next one.☺ *Kasie H.*

Best book I've read in some time. Shows Kidd's love for God, love for wife, family, and the lost. *Sandy B.*

If you have not read Jonnie Whittington's latest book you are missing out. It is awesome! I promise you won't be able to put it down. It touched my heart so much! I loved every bit of it and can't wait for the next book, Kidd's Daughter! *Cheryl B.*

Great book and well written.   *Melvin H.*

Refreshing and captivating! Could hardly put it down!
Joann P.

Just want to tell you how much I enjoyed Kidd and Spitfire Doll. The word that comes to mind is "Wow"! Please let me be one of the first to read, "Kidd's Daughter". I can hardly wait.
Jack H.

Be sure to tell people this exciting book is a true story about your parents. It will touch a lot of people when they know it really happened.
Kevin J.

Just finished your book about Yates and Dollie. Really enjoyed it. Thank you for mentioning my grandmother, Sister Parrish. She was a blessed woman of God.
Anita C.

I finished your book this week and wanted to say that "I loved it"!! I find myself thinking about it often every day and how God miraculously had his hand upon your Mom and Dad. What a testimony and faith builder for us all. I am so looking forward to the next book too. Love you and pray that God will continue to inspire you as you continue to inspire his people.
Pam W.

I just wanted to let you know that I LOVED your book! I could hardly put it down for wondering what would happen next! A great testimony of God's power and ability! Thank you for sharing and please let me know as soon as Kidd's Daughter is available! Thanks again!
Sonya B.

Jonnie, just finished the book and I loved it! Very interesting and well written. What a heritage you have. God Bless!
Tricia J.

It's refreshing to read a story that first is true and second has such a great ending. I personally know the author and Mr. and Mrs. Kidd. I remember hearing some of these stories as a child. It's great to be able to read the rest of the story.   *Jennie H.*

Kidd and Spitfire Doll

Books by Jonnie Whittington

Bible Studies
Building Your House
Wives of the Bible

Biographical Historical Novel
Kidd and Spitfire Doll

Kidd and Spitfire Doll

Jonnie Kidd Whittington

Kidd Family
Series

Book One

HTP
Hidden Treasures
Publishing

Hidden Treasures Publishing

Cover created by Jason Taylor
Editor: Cassie Selleck

Scripture quotations are taken from the King James
Version of the Bible.

To protect the privacy of people in this book some details
and names have been changed.

Library of Congress Cataloging-in-Publication Data
ISBN 978-0-9856986-0-7 (soft cover)
Kidd and Spitfire Doll / Jonnie Kidd Whittington
(Kidd Family series; book one)

Printed in the United States of America

Dedication

Daddy was a Klansman before he became a preacher. I grew up hearing bits and pieces of his and Mama's story - a story of beatings and killings and burning crosses. That was before they found Christ and the baptism of the Holy Spirit. Now, the Pentecostal blessing is the fastest growing segment of Christianity in the world, but a whole generation doesn't know what it was like back in the early days of the 'out pouring' in America. They've never heard of the supernatural experiences that happened in the 1920's and 1930's.

I want to tell them.

Kidd and Spitfire Doll is for this new generation.

Table of Contents

Yates Kidd

1919-1929

From the dust of the earth
God
Created man

Prologue

A red glow from tail lights catches the sailor's attention. He steps out of his car and stands beside a tree as the dark sedan pulls in and parks across the street from the storefront meeting. Doors open. Two shadowy figures wearing pinstriped suits and black fedoras emerge.

Eerie light from the street lamp flashes on a metal object held in the right hand of one of the men, the sailor gasps, swallows, and steps back into the shadows. Beads of perspiration cover his forehead. His feet stick to the spot as the gunman's low growl reveals his intentions for Kidd.

He looks through the building's plate glass window. Hung from black chords, naked light bulbs glare and outline Kidd standing on a makeshift platform – preaching. The sailor holds his breath as the sinister figure with gun pointed strides toward the door of the building . . .

One

1919

Yates Kidd adjusted the strap over his left shoulder to prevent the rifle from knocking against his leg with each step. He cupped his hand above his eyes and stared toward woods that surrounded the house.

Light from the rising sun filtered through dark, bare branches of trees and patches of swirling fog, Yates wondered if he could even see a moving target. Eight-years-old was too young to worry about where the next meal was coming from, but since Pa had taken sick, the three oldest boys took turns providing food for Ma to cook.

The scent of a burning log twitched at Yates' nose. He turned as smoke curled from the chimney of the old home place. One of his two older brothers, either Roby or Gilbert, kindled fire in the hearth to warm the house in time for Ma's biscuit and gravy breakfast.

The two-story frame house had been in the Kidd family for three generations. Yates studied the dark, weathered boards of the house outlined against the pale sky and felt a sense of comfort and security. He quickened his pace and headed for the woods.

Pa said the boys' future was tied up with their

education so Yates kept his ears pealed for the school bell. He wanted to please Pa and be on time, but more than that, he simply loved to learn.

Something rustled in the bushes; Yates grabbed for his gun. A possum emerged from underbrush and wobbled its way across the clearing. Drawing in his breath, Yates lifted the gun to his shoulder and looked down the barrel. He followed the weaving critter, adjusting the frame until the scope was set on the target, the possum centered in the middle of the cross bars. He squeezed the trigger. The piercing blast reverberated through the woods.

"Gotcha!"

Stomping toward the spot, his boots crunched the dry leaves in the scrub. He arrived as the animal lay quivering its last breaths. Yates bent, grabbed it by the tail and stuffed it into his croaker sack. Grinning, he patted the coarse bag, "Supper."

Night fell and the family sat down to steaming bowls of possum stew. Twelve-year-old Roby took a big bite and rubbed his stomach. "This is one good stew, Yates."

Yates smiled, sat taller and held his head high.

"Glad ya' like it."

The next week, the boys had a hard time finding food. Finally, toward the end of the week, Yates' ten-year-old brother Gilbert came upon a whole covey of quail. He tramped home and asked Yates to help him saw up a couple of old boards. They hammered four pieces together to make a big box, attaching one on the front with hinges at the top for a trap door. Yates tied a long piece of string onto a little stick.

The next day after grabbing a couple of Ma's leftover biscuits, the boys trudged back to the site holding the trap between them. Yates carried the stick and string. Crumbling a biscuit Gilbert dropped it on the ground in a straight line that led to the box while Yates broke the other biscuit and scattered it inside the trap. After propping the door up with the stick, the brothers walked away string in hand and hid in the bushes – waiting.

The quail fluttered down, found the crumbs and ate their way inside the trap. When the last one shuffled in, Gilbert yanked the string. The door slammed shut.

"That's it," Yates shouted. The boys dragged the trap full of quail back to the house.

Ma was elated. She had spent the whole morning worrying and wondering if today the boys would find meat for her to cook. Gilbert and Yates helped her clean the quail while six-year-old Denson tried to help, but kept getting under foot. Ma cooked the quail in a big pot of rice, and they all agreed it was a meal fit for a king. That night in spite of Pa's sickness the four brothers joked around the table.

After their laughter died down, Ma said, "See boys, how the Lord provides for His children."

Gilbert piped up with, "The *Lord*! Ma, it was me and Yates who trapped them quail."

Yates and Roby roared at that one and even Ma smiled. "I know son, but the good Lord Himself put them there and showed you where to find them."

"Well, pass me some more of 'em then," Gilbert said and they all laughed again.

When Yates quit laughing his face grew somber as he pondered Ma's statement. He wondered if it was really God who put the quail in their path or just chance. He wasn't sure which.

Denson broke into his pattern of thought by begging to go hunting with the older boys next time, but Ma said he was too young.

Pa thought different. "Josie," he said, "a boy is never too young to learn to provide."

After that, Ma let him go.

Yates loved the days the four brothers hunted together. On those rare occasions, they ventured deep into the woodland. When they were out of earshot and knew Ma and Pa couldn't see them, they divided up.

"I'm a Cowboy," Roby called out.

"Me, too." Denson stood beside his big brother.

"Yates, you and Gilbert are Indians." Roby gave the orders.

Yates and Gilbert immediately put their hand over their mouth and began an Indian war whoop, bobbing and running after the two Cowboys.

Denson yelled back at them, "You redskins can't catch us." He and Roby ducked behind a huge tree, aimed their guns and began to shoot at the Indians.

Yates and Gilbert dipped, shot toward the tree the cowboys hid behind, and then took cover at the back side of a tall bush.

Back and forth they darted through the woods, yelling and ducking in and out behind the trees just in the nick of time, while bullets zinged past their heads. They whooped and hollered and shot at each other until a bullet came so close to Yates he smelled the fire and felt wind from it blow his hair. He jumped back laughing. "You nearly got me that time, Cowboy."

All at once, Roby didn't think it was funny anymore. "All right boys this game is over." He was in charge again.

"Aw, Roby we're just having fun." Yates rubbed his forehead where the bullet barely missed.

"That was too close for comfort, Yates, and you know it."

"A miss is as good as a mile," Yates bantered.

"Boys, I said we're done. Let's find some meat for supper."

The boys argued back, but finally hushed. They tiptoed through the trees until they spotted a rabbit. Each boy aimed and shot and each one claimed it was his bullet that hit the target. Roby settled it, picked up the animal and the brothers started for home.

"Don't none of you say a word about our Cowboy and Indian game or Pa'll give us all a lickin'."

"He's too sick to whip anybody," Gilbert said.

When they saw Ma and handed her the rabbit, she looked at them as if they wore halos. None the wiser, she thought her angelic boys had hunted wild game all day.

In bed that night Yates remembered the bullet that glazed his forehead. Mrs. Beulah, his Sunday school teacher had told him that we all have a guardian angel to watch over us sent directly from God. *Maybe my guardian angel kept that bullet from hitting me* was his last thought before he drifted off to sleep.

That fall Roby quit school to hold down a-full-time job diminishing his trips to hunt. He took his newfound responsibility seriously and the younger boys were quick to complain.

Gilbert told him, "You been passing out orders like somebody put you in charge around here. Pa ain't dead, ya know."

Yates agreed with Gilbert, but didn't think it was his place to tell him, so he kept quiet.

Ma and Pa were upset about Roby missing out on his schooling, but there was no way around it. Pa wasn't able to work. He couldn't cough every breath and teach boys and girls all day.

After Pa quit teaching school, he became a night watchman. The first evening before he went to work, the boys gathered around admiring his new blue uniform. They thought he was a policeman. Instead, he sat in a little building and once an hour went outside to make sure everything was all right. Now, too weak to work at all, the boys took up the slack. Ma's hands were full doctoring Pa, tending to two baby girls, and trying to feed four growing boys. She was glad to have the boys' willing help.

During the summer months, with Pa's guidance, the boys helped Ma plant and hoe a garden behind the house. They picked the vegetables and Ma canned them in clear glass mason jars. After boiling them in a large pot, she set them on the porcelain cabinet top to cool.

Throughout the evening, Yates heard a ping as one by one the lids sealed. The sound assured him of food for the long winter.

One day Ma sent him to the cellar for a jar of green

beans. While he was down there, he noticed the supply of vegetables had dwindled to nearly nothing. That wasn't what worried Yates most though, what they had or didn't have to eat. No. What worried him most was whether Pa lived or died.

* * *

Early one morning, before the sun lit the sky, Yates awoke to the gurgling sound of Pa's cough and Ma's frantic call for help. Yates' heart pounded and he dreaded what waited. Jumping out of bed he ran into the next room.

The dim glow of the kerosene lamp resting on the dresser cast Pa's shadow on the wall. He sat on the side of the bed coughing while dark red blood erupted from his mouth and into the chamber pot. The blood splattered on his feet and the floor. Yates blinked the sleep out of his eyes and stood at Pa's side. He had seen this before, more times than he could count.

"Get me some rags, Yates," Ma said.

He ran to the chiffonier and grabbed out a handful. When the hemorrhage stopped Ma wiped the blood from Pa's feet, and then helped him lie back on their iron bedstead.

"You can't go on like this, Neuby. There has to be something we can do."

When he could talk again, Pa answered, "There is. I know you don't want to leave your family, Josie, but the doctor says . . ."

"I don't want to move to Florida." Ma's lips were in a straight line as her eyes silently pled with her husband.

Pa held her gaze for a moment before closing his eyes. "I don't want to die," he sighed. His face matched the muslin sheets.

Ma's chin quivered. After a long pause, she said, "It'll take a while to pack for eight of us; I'd better start today."

Pa's voice was barely a whisper, "I'll go first." He rested. "Send for you and the young'uns when I find a place to live."

Yates stood gaping, wondering what in the world lay ahead.

"Don't stand there with your mouth open, Yates," Ma said. "Help me clean up this mess." Shuddering at the odor of blood, she bent and wiped it off the floor then handed the dirty rags and potty to Yates.

"Do something with these."

His breath came out like smoke as Yates carried them outside into the cold winter morning and tossed the rags into a bucket. He hurried to the outhouse and emptied the chamber pot bringing it back to the pump stand. As soon as the sun melted the frozen hand pump, he would come back and fill the container with water to soak the rags and rinse the porcelain slop-jar.

He stood on the porch and stared out at the woods. Naked limbs on the trees appeared grotesque and desolate on that frigid December day making him feel alone and scared. When he slipped back into the house, the dilapidated slat door groaned on its hinges, and icy fingers of frost seeped through the cracks.

Yates walked into the bedroom as Ma piled heavy scrap quilts on top of Pa to stop his shivering. Written all over her face was compassion for her husband; love and concern showed in her soft brown eyes.

"I do worry about you going off, Neuby. I 'spect you aren't in any condition to travel alone. How about taking one of the boys with you?"

Pa's chin finally stopped quivering enough to say, "I'll take the train. That won't be hard on me."

"But you need somebody with you," Ma insisted.

"I could go, Pa," Yates volunteered.

"No, Son. You need to stay here and help your Ma."

"But Neuby, you need one of the bigger boys . . ."

"Josie, listen to me," Pa's voice was stern. "You need the boys more than I do." He rested a spell. When he spoke again his voice was soft, almost gentle. "You'd have an awful time bringing all these young'uns on the train without the boys to help you."

"I know you're right, Neuby, but I still worry."

Pa patted her arm, "Don't fret. God'll take care of me."

Baby Mary whimpered from the corner. Ma picked her up to let her nurse.

The next day Ma helped Pa get ready for the train trip; she starched his blue shirt until it was stiff as a board, then dampened and rolled it into a ball. While the flat iron heated on the wood cook stove, she laid the shirt out on a table. When she thought the iron was hot enough, she wet her finger with a little spit, and touched it to the iron. It sizzled like a firecracker. She pressed until the shirt was smooth and crisp.

Pa put it on his frail body and the color of the shirt made his eyes look bluer than the sky. He stepped into his dark trousers and Ma hooked up his suspenders.

In spite of his weight loss, he looked handsome and

distinguished with his white hair fresh and clean. Pa's hair was once black as coal, but turned white when he was only twenty-five. Yates only remembered him with white hair.

Pa, with his medium build and height, was strong until he ruptured his lungs while cranking a Model T Ford. He told the boys, "When you get old enough to drive, be careful. Those cars are dangerous the way they kick back while you turn the crank."

Yates admired his Pa and listened to everything he said. His Pa was smart, not only in learning, but in working, too. Besides being a school teacher and night watchman, he knew how to farm and build. Yates longed to be like him.

Every day, when Pa had a spare minute, Yates watched him pull out his pencil stub, open his pocket knife, and shave a new point on the end of his pencil. When it was sharp enough he wrote numbers on the pad he carried.

Yates knew that he was figuring again, and dreaming.

He figured things like how many rows of a crop he should plant to make enough vegetables to feed the family. He figured how big he ought to build each room in the new house and what the materials would cost. And money – he always figured on how to bring in more money.

When the coughing started, Pa laid aside his pencil and pad. His shoulders sagged and his blue eyes drooped with fatigue. The doctor told him, "Mr. Kidd, you have a big problem with your lungs. You need to move to Florida where the sun shines every day. I believe the sun will help you get well."

Yates wanted to see Pa get well. If it meant his

family had to leave their home in North Carolina and move to Florida, he was willing. They had moved many times before and Yates figured once more wouldn't make much difference. But this move would take them hundreds of miles away. It seemed to him they were going to a whole different world. According to a book he read at school, it was a world that was surrounded by water and palm trees, a place where alligators roamed; A world where, as far as he could tell, they didn't know another living soul.

* * *

The day of Pa's trip, Yates and all the family went to the train station. Before he left, Pa touched each one of the boys on the head. He stopped in front of the oldest one.

"Now, Roby, you're the man of the house while I'm gone." Pa's eyes glistened.

"Yessir." Roby shook Pa's hand. "I'll take care of everything, Pa. Don't you worry none. Go on to Florida and get well."

Pa nodded. He hugged Ma and the two baby girls. "I'll send for all of you soon, Josie."

He looked Yates square in the eyes. "Help your Ma, Yates."

"Yessir."

Pulling his winter coat up tight, Pa grasped the valise which contained a few of his belongings, and boarded the train. The big engine gave an ear splitting screech as it started. Yates' heart raced. White steam flowed out in big cloud-like puffs as the train pulled out chugging and tooting. Billows of black smoke rolled above it.

Yates chased it a long ways, smiling and waving a

last goodbye to Pa, who leaned his head back on the wooden slat seat and stared out the window to watch Yates run. He was barely able to wave.

Yates loved his pale, weak Pa and hated to see him go. Pa's last words rang in his ears, *help your Ma*. He was plenty big enough for that and loved his Ma, too. He would do as Pa said.

As soon as the train rounded a bend and faded from sight, he ran back to the station. Ma sat on the bench with his baby sister Mary on her lap and Virgie toddling at her feet. Roby, Gilbert, and Denson stood huddled to one side. Tears streamed down Ma's face and she bit her lip. Her eyes were glued to the spot where Pa boarded the train. Yates knew she thought the same thing as him – *they may never see Pa alive again.*

Two

Pa dragged his suitcase onto the train. Exhausted and breathless, he fell into a seat near the door. After wiping his tears on a handkerchief, he stared out the window watching Josie and the children until the back of the train blocked his view.

Yates ran along beside the train, waving. Pa watched him run; glad that Yates' strong legs carried him easily. He swallowed the lump in his throat, and told himself that he was doing the right thing; although, now that his plan was in motion, he wasn't so sure.

When the train chugged around a bend in the track and Yates turned back to the station, Pa glanced around him. He noticed a man about his age eyeing him curiously from across the aisle.

"Where ya headin'?" asked the man in the straw hat.

"Florida." Pa gasped.

"Sure nuf. That's where I'm a-goin'."

He pulled at the straps of overalls that looked as if they'd been through many a Monday wash. "What part of Florida?"

"Tampa."

"That ain't far from Lakeland where I live."

Pa did his best to reply, but weakened by the conversation, began to cough into his handkerchief.

"That sure sounds bad. Are you able to travel clear to Tampa?"

From behind the handkerchief, Pa managed a weak, muffled, "I believe so." He took a deep breath and tried not to cough again. "My doctor thinks the Florida sun will help me get well."

"Well, if it don't, I know something that *will* help for sure."

"What's that?"

"Prayer – that is if you believe in it."

"I certainly do."

"If you like, I'll take you to Durant. It's just a little town not far from Tampa." Mr. Wilson said.

"What's in Durant?"

"A tabernacle with a revival in full swing. This woman, Amy Simple McPherson, preaches every night and prays for the sick. Lot of folks getting healed." He paused and looked at Pa for a long moment. "You could get well, you know – if you believe."

Pa listened with his eyes wide.

The man's name was Charles Wilson. Pa told him his name, Cephas Neuby Kidd. The two conversed off and on during the rest of the long trip. Mr. Wilson replayed healings he witnessed in the revival meeting, and Pa wondered if there was anything to all Mr. Wilson's talk. He hadn't heard of anything like it, but somehow it gave him a tiny ray of hope.

The trip went better with someone to talk to and as the train pulled into the Tampa station, Mr. Wilson asked Pa where he was staying.

"Well, now, I don't rightly know. Thought I'd check out one of them boarding houses." Pa turned his head and coughed; Mr. Wilson saw blood on his handkerchief.

"If you ain't got a place to stay, you need to come home with me. My wife'll fix us some good supper and you can lie down and rest."

"I can't impose on you like that."

"We'd be glad to have you."

When the train came to a full stop, Mr. Wilson grabbed Pa's suitcase and whisked him off to his house in Lakeland. After a good hot meal of fried fish, grits, warm buttered biscuits to sop in cane syrup, and sweet iced tea, he led him to a clean bed. "Get you some sleep and when you feel up to it, I'll take you to the revival."

Pa rested that night. The next evening Charles Wilson and his wife drove him to the Durant Pleasant Grove Tabernacle. When they walked under the brush arbor, people smiled and shook hands with them. Pa didn't care that the homemade wooden benches felt hard as a rock against his spine, or that the floor under his feet was curly bits of sawdust. He felt more warmth with these people than in any other place.

Pa told his new friends about his family waiting in North Carolina and in a few days they found them a house. Before he was in Florida two weeks, Pa sent for his family.

* * *

"It'll be OK, it'll be OK, it'll be OK." The clacking wheels of the moving train echoed in Yates' mind as it sped toward

Florida. He wondered if Pa heard the same message two weeks earlier and felt as Yates did - they were going to the land of sunshine, the land of hope.

He sat behind Ma, close enough to help her with his two little sisters. Virgie was three and Mary a little over a month old. He remembered the day little Mary was born and weighed two and a half pounds, so tiny she slept in a shoebox. Now she was big enough to take a train ride on Ma's lap.

Yates felt proud when he looked at his Ma with her thick, dark hair pulled back neatly in a bun. He thought she inherited her good looks from her great, great grandmother, a Cherokee Indian Princess. Ma was a gentle woman, patient and kind with an optimistic nature. Yates loved the twinkle that lit her soft brown eyes when she smiled. And the merry way she laughed even in the face of problems. Nothing pulled her down, she simply laughed it off; That is until Pa got sick. Then she began to lose interest in things. Since his illness, Ma had quit laughing and writing her poetry.

Yates leaned up in the seat. "Ma," he said, "did you bring your letter?"

"Yates, you need to forget about that letter. I'm not accepting the position."

"Did you tell him that?"

"I mailed a letter today."

"Can I read it again? Please."

Ma reached into her pocketbook and drew out a ragged envelope. "Here."

Yates opened the letter. Across the top of the official stationery he read, "From the Office of the

Governor of the State of North Carolina."

"Wow!" he said. "Imagine that! The Governor!" His eyes fairly danced as Yates read aloud for what seemed to Ma like the hundredth time,

"Dear Mrs. Kidd,

Recently, I was advised to review your published work. After a thorough study, I feel that your poetry about our lovely state is an asset to us. I hereby appoint you, Josephine Lola (Sheffield) Kidd, Poet Laureate of North Carolina.

Please send a letter of confirmation of your acceptance or rejection. It is my sincere desire that your answer will be in the affirmative.

It was signed by the Governor.

"Why won't you do it, Ma? "

"Yates Kidd, you know good and well I can't go traipsing all over the state with all my responsibility. Who would tend to you young'uns? Besides, we'll be living in Florida now."

"But, you sure do write good poems, Ma."

"Thank you." Ma looked at Yates and after a brief pause continued, "That only happens now and then, son. I might not think of anything when they called on me to write a poem for a special occasion. Sure wouldn't want to let anybody down."

Yates thought he saw sadness in her eyes when she turned back to take the letter and put it in her purse.

Looking out the train window, Yates watched the trees speeding past as if they raced with time. He wondered why they ran in the opposite direction, like they were beating it back to their old home. Maybe, they were trying to show him how the same train that took them away could also bring them back.

All this thinking made him want a cigarette. Ever since he was six-years-old, he slipped behind the barn whenever he got a chance, to roll his own smoke. Of course, Pa tanned his hide when he caught Yates, but it hadn't stopped him. Pa and other farmers in the area where they lived grew tobacco. Why shouldn't he smoke it? Since no tobacco field or barn was on the train, he struggled to put his mind on something else.

Yates thought about Pa and Gilbert, his brother. When Pa still had his health, he taught his boys how to do things right because he wanted them to succeed. He whipped them for the same reason. Yates had heard him repeat the words time and time again, "You need to learn and amount to something." He knew Pa meant well, but Gilbert didn't share the same opinion. Yates thought Pa's discipline wasn't as fair as it could be.

At times, when Pa spoke to Gilbert, his tone changed as if Gilbert grated on an invisible secret nerve. Pa corrected him about every little thing he did or said, and blamed Gilbert for misdeeds of the other boys. Yates wondered if every family had a scapegoat like Gilbert – one who took the blame for all.

The razor strap whippings Pa gave Gilbert made him more stubborn and rebellious. Before Pa got sick, he was a serious-minded man with a gruff voice which often made him sound angry when he wasn't. Yates understood that, but not Gilbert. No matter how much Yates explained this, Gilbert still took Pa's scolding to heart.

"He ain't mad at ya, Gib." Yates told him one day

when Pa told Gilbert to catch a stray cow.

"Sure sounds like it to me." Gilbert clinched his jaw and stuck his hands in his pockets.

"Na, it's just his voice," Yates said.

"Don't sound like that when he talks to you." Gilbert turned his head away.

"Yeah he does, I jest don't pay it no attention. Jest do what he says 'cause I know it's his voice. Besides, he don't feel good now, sick as he is."

"Just the same, I'm leaving home soon as I can. Ain't putting up with his fussing with me much longer." Gilbert hung his head and shuffled off.

Yates sure hoped he wouldn't leave anytime soon. He knew Pa would need their help in Florida, more than ever.

About noontime, Ma opened the basket of lunch she packed for the trip and spread peanut butter on her delicious homemade biscuits. Yates begged her to let him pass them out. As he did, Yates felt he was helping Ma just as Pa said and that made him feel like an important member of the family.

Roby cut the apples Ma brought and they all ate a slice. Pa raised peanuts and, before they left home, Ma parched some in the oven. While Yates passed them around, the porter appeared with water and milk. They thanked him for his kindness and generosity and Ma for her tasty food.

The full stomach and the repetitious chug of the train as it rumbled over the tracks with a gentle side to side motion lulled Yates. His eyes grew heavy, but he forced himself to keep them open. He couldn't waste time with sleep. He might miss something. "Roby," he said, "tell us a story."

"Which one you wanna hear?"

"The one about the Christmas program at the Baptist Church, remember? You were real little."

Roby looked around at the family and began. "Well, I was seven. That was way before Grandma and Grandpa left us the old homestead, where we live now. . . I mean, where we just left.

"Anyhow it was Christmas time and we had to move 'cause the owner of the house we lived in threw us out."

Ma broke into the story. "Wait a minute Roby, the owner didn't throw us out. He needed the house for some of his kin."

"Yeah, that's right; he needed it for his kin. Anyhow, Pa searched high and low for us a place. Couldn't find nothing but an old shack. It had one room, and a built-on shed for the kitchen. That creepy old place was full of rats and bats and spider webs.

"Late in the afternoon, Pa and his friend loaded up everything we owned on the man's wagon and his mule pulled it down the road. They got to the old shanty 'bout sundown, and piled our stuff in the middle of the room. Pa hurried back to get us: Ma, Gilbert, Yates and me. Yates, you were 'bout two then.

"It was a cold night in December and real dark. Pa lighted a lantern, and we walked the mile to the house shivering all the way. The little bit of light from Pa's swinging lantern cast shadows on the bushes and trees. More than once, I thought I saw a creature lurking out there and I heard um, too. Me and Gilbert stayed close together, right behind Ma. She and Pa took turns totin' you, Yates.

"Pa led the way and finally we got to the cabin door. He pushed it open; I can still hear the screech the hinges made. The odor from cooked, rancid, fat-back meat, and rotten wood, mixed with body odor from whoever slept there last, rushed out the door to greet us. Pa stepped inside and held his lantern high above his head.

"I can still see that picture: The old dark walls covered with dust and cobwebs, and Pa, with his body outlined in the dim light of the oil lantern, looking real worried as he gazed at all our stuff scattered around him. There were boxes running over with pots, pans, dishes, and a big ole pile of quilts.

"Pa told Ma that it was too big a job for that night. He said we'd go on up to Uncle Lon's and spend the night with them. At that time, they had four girls and one boy.

They made down beds on the floor for us young'uns, and gave Pa and Ma their company bed.

"Next morning, we looked out and everything was covered with snow. It was fun playing and making a snowman 'till we found out Pa had pneumonia. The doctor came and said he couldn't leave 'till he was well.

"Five long weeks we stayed at uncle Lon's. At first they treated us good, but with seven young'uns and four grown-ups the house soon felt too small, and we cousins got into a few disagreements. We had worn out our welcome, but Pa was sick and there was nothing else we could do.

"Christmas was near and the local church was having a program. Our cousins learned parts for it and the lady in charge wanted me to memorize some verses to recite. I told her that I already knew some and she said that was good, but she didn't stop and listen to them.

"Christmas Eve was my big night. I felt like I was breaking into show business. All the other children said their speeches, some were loud and clear and some bashful like. The audience clapped for all of them.

"I was last on the program, and my heart hammered in my chest as I mounted the platform. There I stood, facing a staring audience. This is the verse I said, loud and clear, in a little Baptist church, December 24, 1914:

I went to the river and I couldn't get across.
I had nothing but an old blind hoss.
 He bucked and he reared and he curled up his tail,
 And he carried me across on his big toe nail.

"That audience went wild with applause. It sounded like sweet music to my ears." Roby ended his story and looked around to see the response. The family howled with laughter. Even Ma chuckled regardless of her concern for Pa.

After they quieted down, Roby continued, "After that night I want to be an actor, maybe even go to Hollywood."

"Me, too," Denson said. "When I grow up, I *am* going out there and be a cowboy in picture shows."

"Not me," mumbled Gilbert, "I ain't going to Hollywood, but I'm going somewhere."

Although Yates loved talking to his family, he felt inferior to his big brother Roby and too timid to be in front of a big audience. "I couldn't never tell a story good as Roby." He sighed and sat back in his seat. He figured he'd just work hard at something. Maybe he'd raise chickens or cows in Florida. That would give people food to eat. He'd like that.

When they all settled down again, Yates dug out a handful of peanuts stuffed in his pocket.

"Hey Gib," he called to his brother, across the aisle, as he chewed.

"What?"

"You ain't gonna be a North Carolina 'Tar Heel' no more." He laughed and threw a peanut at him.

Gilbert caught the peanut and threw it back. "What you mean, Hoot?" he said, using Yates' nickname.

"You'll be a 'Cracker' when we get to Florida."

"Don't you call me no 'Cracker'!" Gilbert reached across the aisle and punched Yates on the arm. "You know what you'll be, don't ya? You'll be an alligator." He put his hands together at the wrist and snapped them like a giant mouth opening and closing.

"No, I won't, neither." Yates jerked his head and shoulders up. "I'm gonna be a Florida Cracker and proud of it," He stuck out his chest.

"Ha, if you're a Cracker a gator will pro'ly eat ya alive. I hear they're everywhere down there." Gilbert put his foot on the back of the seat in front of him and leaned his head against the hard slats behind him.

As they neared Tampa, they passed acres of trees covered with oranges. The only time the family ate oranges was Christmas day. Seeing them grow plentifully on trees made Yates hungry.

"Look at them oranges, Gib." Yates poked him on the arm and pointed. "Let's hop off this train and pick us one. Think we can catch up to it and get back on?" He could almost taste the sweetness and feel the juice drip off his chin.

Roby heard him. He changed from the story teller back to boss. "You'll do no such thing," he said sternly. "Pa put me in charge of this trip and you'll do as I say. What ails you, Hoot, talking like that?" He glanced toward Ma, then back to Yates and lowered his voice, "You ain't gonna worry Ma. She's got her hands full with the babies and Pa sick and all."

"Sure, Roby. I was just kiddin'."

"Cause your last name's Kidd don't mean you have to kid all the time. Now settle down Hoot and quit your nonsense." With that, Roby turned and looked out the window as the train passed another orange grove.

Leaning back in the seat, Yates forgot about Roby trying to boss him around. Instead, he thought about all the fruit trees. "Looks like Florida is gonna be a real good place to live, huh Gib?"

"Yeah, I reckon."

Yates wondered about life in Florida and if Pa would get well. He hoped they lived close to woods where the boys could hunt for food. He figured things would work out somehow. They usually did. Ma always said, "If we help others, God'll take care of us."

The train was still telling him, "It'll be OK," when it pulled into the station at Tampa. The loud recurring bump and the squeal of metal against metal each time the cars hit one another as the train ground to a halt, notified Yates that the trip was over.

"Hey Gib, we're in Florida. Better watch out for the

alligators." Yates punched him as they hopped off the train.

Roby helped Ma with baby Mary and Yates grabbed his little sister Virgie's hand. Gilbert and Denson retrieved the luggage. They had arrived.

Pa's new friend, Mr. Wilson, stood on the platform to meet the family. The look on his face alerted Ma that something was wrong. When she questioned him, he said, "Come over here, Mrs. Kidd." They walked a few steps out of earshot of the children.

"Mr. Kidd's cough is worse," he said softly. "Plus, he got some bad news from the doctor down here."

The little bit of color left in Ma's face, drained. "What's that?"

"Well, he mentioned something about Tuberculosis. There ain't no cure for that. It looks like, Mr. Kidd's gonna have to trust God to help him."

Ma's hand flew up to her throat. She gasped, "No! Not TB."

He leaned toward her and whispered, "Don't let the children hear, and don't go worrying yourself, Mrs. Kidd, I'm still believin' God for his healing."

Ma nodded looking more worried and tired than ever.

Yates felt the Florida sun, warm on his face. He didn't know if it had helped Pa yet, but thought it was bound to since it shined brighter here than it had in North Carolina. The sky didn't look washed out like it did up there. It was a darker blue and grass looked more vivid green. Palmetto trees with their big pointed fronds, lined the street.

"Hey, Gib, let's go barefoot." Yates stepped out of his shoes and peeled off his socks. The soil was loose, not firm like the red North Carolina clay. He wiggled his toes in the hot, blond sand. It felt good to his bare skin. "I do like it here and Daddy *is* gonna get well," he said to himself as much as to his brother Gilbert.

Yates didn't know then, but across town lived a little girl named Dollie . . .

Three

Goose bumps rose on Yates' arms and the back of his neck as he followed his family into the Pentecostal Holiness Tabernacle. They found empty seats in the middle of the brush arbor and stood in front of them, all in a row. With service already started people were on their feet, clapping their hands and singing with all their might. A woman moved up and down on the piano bench as she banged out the notes. Her playing along with the congregation's singing gave the songs themselves a life of their own – different from anything Yates ever heard.

The man in front of Yates waved his hand in the air as if flagging down a train, sweat poured from his forehead. His wife, bouncing a baby on her shoulder, gently moved to the music. The soft smell of baby powder reached Yates' nose as the swaying infant gazed at him over his mother's shoulder.

Yates smiled. The baby returned a toothless grin, and buried his face in his mother's neck. Peeking out at him again, he wrapped his fingers around one of the curly tendrils dangling from the thick hair swept up on top of his mother's head, then beamed back at Yates once more.

At the end of the row, a woman was in the aisle. She twirled and danced creating a little cloud at her feet from the sawdust floor.

Yates elbowed Gilbert standing next to him, "You ever seen anything like that in church?" He pointed.

Gilbert looked and before he replied they both gaped as the dancing woman's head jerked and hairpins began to fall. She glided and turned and sprang up and down until there wasn't a single pin left. When the pins stopped peppering down and lay all around in the sawdust, wavy auburn hair flowed down to her waist. Light, from the setting sun, filtered through the open side of the Tabernacle. It illuminated her hair and shone on her face. Yates couldn't tell whether the ethereal light was from the sun, or coming from inside her. Either way it made her look, for all the world, like an angel.

Yates rubbed his arms. "You feel that, Gib?" he whispered. "Reckon what it is?"

Gilbert shrugged. "I don't know."

Roby put his finger to his lips, said, "Shhh," and gave the boys a stern look.

Although, Ma was raised a proud Methodist and Pa a staunch Baptist, they joined right in the service. Ma sang and Pa patted his foot to the beat of the music. The next time Yates looked their way, Ma was clapping her hands, but Pa sat on the bench breathing heavy, his face pale.

After a few songs, the music changed to a slow one and goose bumps started up again on Yates. When he looked at Ma this time, tears ran down her face. He elbowed Gilbert. "What ails Ma?"

Gilbert shrugged, glanced at her anxiously, and

turned back to say something when Roby told them to pipe down or he would tell.

When the preacher finally stood to preach, the sun had gone down. Two men lit kerosene lanterns that hung on ropes tied to the ceiling beams. Dim light from the lamps cast a soft glow over the faces of men and women gathered under the brush arbor tabernacle.

The preacher was a large man with a booming voice. He took his text from Revelation 20:15, and read, "Whosoever was not found written in the book of life was cast into the lake of fire." He looked around at the crowd and paused before he began his sermon. "God has prepared a wonderful place called heaven for those who believe in his son, Jesus," his voice rose slightly. "But for those who do not believe, he has prepared a very different place. My message tonight is on Hell. And there's a lot of ways you can get there."

Yates and Gilbert sat up straight, eyes wide, waiting to hear his next words.

"Liquor," his voice thundered. "Makes no difference if it's moonshine, or store bought, it will damn your soul to hell." He banged his fist on the wooden stand in front of him. The boys jumped.

"The Bible says in Proverbs not to look on wine when it is red and moves itself in the cup. Strong drink is a mocker and whosoever is deceived thereby is not wise."

Gilbert swallowed and looked pale.

"And don't be deceived by cigarettes." He yelled the word *cigarettes*, pounded again on the table, and looked straight at Yates who squirmed on the bench.

"If you think you can smoke them devil sticks and

go to heaven, you're dead wrong, son."

Yates' heart raced and he broke out in a cold sweat.

"You'll end up in the pits of a devil's hell," the preacher continued. "And you'll be smoking all right . . . but it won't be cigarettes burning . . . it'll be your soul."

As quickly as his rant began, his tone softened and a group sang quietly in the background while he made his appeal.

"Hell was not created for you, my children. God created it for the devil and his angels. You don't have to go there. God made a way to avoid it by sending his son Jesus to die on a cross. He paid the price for your sins. Give them up to Jesus." His voice was almost a whisper, but each word distinct. "If you want to escape this terrible place called hell, come to this altar and repent of your sins. You can lay them right here on the mourner's bench." He pointed toward the low, wooden, backless bench at the front.

"I beg of you," he sobbed, "accept Jesus as your Savior." Compassion colored his voice as he said, "Come on, now. Come to Jesus."

People came. Running and wailing, they knelt at the wooden altar. One man laid a pack of cigarettes on it. The preacher walked over, talked to the man, and prayed with him. He picked up the pack and gave them back to the man who shouted and flung them on the ground. He stomped them screaming, "I'm delivered." Then he took off running, his shirttail flapped as he jogged around the inside of the tabernacle, sawdust flying. The crowd erupted with shouts of "Hallelujah!"

Caught up in the excitement, Yates felt something

tug at his insides. With goose bumps on his arms again, he stood holding on to the back of the seat in front of him. He wanted to go to the altar, but couldn't make his feet move, so he sat down and watched to see what would happen next.

The Kidd family went to the revival night after night. Ma told the boys at supper every evening to get washed up and be ready to go. She enjoyed the services more and more. Though Pa was getting weaker, he said he didn't want to miss a single service in case that was the night he would get his healing.

The preacher announced one night, "My sermon tonight is on Divine Healing." Yates looked down the row at Pa who shifted in his seat and sat up real straight looking right at the preacher.

"Open your Bible and let's look at Matthew 8:16." The man's strong voice carried, past the back row, to those standing outside. "When the evening was come, they brought unto him many that were possessed with devils; and he cast out the spirits with his word, and healed all that were sick."

"This verse makes it clear that the devil tries to take over your life." He swung his head back and forth looking over the crowd. "It says that some were possessed; that means the devil controlled them. To others," he pointed his finger, "he brought sickness. But its God's will to kick the devil out of your life and sickness right along with it." He raised his foot in the air and kicked.

A man shouted, "Amen."

A woman nodded her head and said softly, "That's

right, Brother."

"I want you to think about the word ALL." The preacher looked around, came down from the platform and thrust his Bible toward a young man sitting on the front row. "Brother, do you believe this book is the word of God?"

The man nodded and said, "Amen, Brother."

"Do you believe it's true?" He shook his Bible.

"Yes, I do."

"Do you believe the word *all* means everyone who came to him?"

"Amen!" The young man stood and waved his hand. "I believe it."

"It says here, He healed ALL that were sick." Dancing a little jig, the preacher continued, "That means you. If you're sick, come up here and get healed."

Pa made a beeline for the front. Several others outran him and stood waiting. The preacher went down the line, laying hands on each one's head, and commanded the sickness to come out of them. One woman screamed and shook all over. Some put their hands in the air with tears streaming down their faces. Others danced around. Pa just stood there. Nothing happened to him. When he came back to his seat, his shoulders sagged more than ever. He looked as disappointed as Yates felt.

Pa didn't have much to say for the next few days. Ma encouraged him to continue going to the meeting. Several nights later the preacher read his text in Acts 2:4, "And they were all filled with the Holy Ghost and began to speak in tongues as the Spirit gave them utterance."

"The Holy Ghost is real," he boomed. "The same

thing that happened on the day of Pentecost is happening today." He paused to let his words sink in then continued, "Just last week I received word from a traveling minister that people in California, Tennessee and North Carolina are speaking in tongues. The Holy Ghost is being poured out all around. Some of you have already received, but others are fighting it."

He took out his neatly folded white handkerchief and wiped perspiration from his cheeks and chin. "This experience is a gift that God wants you to have. The gift will enable you to *live holy*," he thundered, "and give you a desire to *help people*." His voice grew softer as he started his appeal, "If you want to receive, come to the front and ask God for the gift of the Holy Ghost."

Yates perked up his ears at that because he liked to help people, but he didn't know about the living holy part. He wasn't ready for all that.

Ma was. She walked to the altar at the front of the tabernacle. The preacher came over and put his hand on her head. She fell backwards to the sawdust floor. Yates thought she had passed out and was hurt, but he learned later that she was slain in the Spirit. She told him when he questioned her, "Yates it didn't pain me a bit. I didn't even feel the sawdust floor when I hit." She also said that while lying there, she had a vision of Pa getting his healing.

That night, it seemed to Yates, she would never get up. She kept her eyes closed and spoke in other tongues for hours. After that experience, she was different, more like her old self. Ma started laughing again.

That same night, while Ma was seeing the vision of Pa getting well, three preachers anointed him with olive oil, laid hands on him and prayed and prayed. Finally after a long time Pa began to shake and jump up and down. Quick as lightening flashes, his color changed. When he walked back to where the family sat, his face was glowing pink, and he held his shoulders up straight. They knew something was different.

The next week, he returned for an examination. The doctor came back in the room with two sets of x-rays in his hands. Looking back and forth from one to the other he frowned.

"What's wrong?" Pa shifted uneasily on the chair.

The doctor held them before the light and looked at the name again. "You are Mr. C. N. Kidd, aren't you?"

"Yes. What is it, Doctor?"

"We need to do this test again."

"Why is that?"

"There's a mistake here. These films don't match the first ones we made."

"It's not a mistake," Pa said beaming.

"But the new ones show a set of clear lungs. There's not a scar from a rupture or a trace of Tuberculosis on them."

"I know," Pa said calmly. "God healed me."

The doctor scratched his head. "I've heard of this kind of thing happening but this is my first time to witness it. Wouldn't have believed it if I hadn't seen it with my own eyes." He pointed at the x-rays and added softly, "I'd call this a miracle."

Pa raced home with the good report. When he told them that the doctor gave him a clean bill of health his family was so happy they whooped and hollered. Even Ma laughed out loud when she grabbed Pa around the neck. He kissed her and said he felt like a brand new man. The family had their Pa back.

"Roby, you and Denson go get all my medicine and bring it here." He looked at each one of the boys. "Gilbert, get a shovel. Yates, help him dig a hole out back. Make it deep enough to bury all these bottles. I don't need any more medicine."

Yates grinned and ran to do the task Pa had assigned. Gilbert followed.

Roby hung back "Are you sure you want to do this, Pa?" he questioned.

"Yes, I'm sure." Pa smiled "I'm healed, son."

Little by little, his strength returned until Pa was as strong as ever. He moved the family to Baum, a place not too far away and known for its rich farmland. Becoming a sharecropper, he planted watermelons, cucumbers and green peppers. Pa said he'd never grow tobacco again.

In the mornings, while getting ready to work in the field, Pa was so happy to be well that he sang. As he walked behind the horse and held the plow that turned the dark rich soil, the family heard him singing all the way to the house:

"I'm going a long, o'er-flowing with song,
    The sin-clouds all rolled away."
When Yates ran out to the field to take him a drink of cold water, Pa was still singing:

"The heavenly Dove is bending above,
    To cheer me from day to day."
Pa stopped the horse at the end of each straight row,

took a piece of cloth, from his pocket and wiped the sweat from his forehead. Then he raised one hand and hollered out thanks to God for his healing. He turned the horse around, started a new row and another round of singing,

"I'm working and singing,
Ever trusting and clinging
To the wonderful Friend above:
And I know He will keep me
When the storm-wave doth sweep me,
I am happy in His great love."

In the evening the family heard his song before they saw him heading in for supper. After the meal, he walked out on the front porch, sat in his chair and sang into the night sky:

"I've a song in my heart,
May it never depart."

Pa still had his gruff voice, but God had mellowed it.

It was good to hear Ma's soft chuckle and see the twinkle back in her eyes when she said quietly to the boys, "Pa's become a regular song bird." Then she hummed along with him, her eyes shining, as she continued her chores.

"Ma," Yates said, "I thought we moved to Florida for the sun to make Pa well."

"The Son did make him well, Yates."

"Huh?" Yates looked puzzled.

"God's only begotten Son."

Yates nodded, "Oh, yeah." A grin covered his whole face.

* * *

One night, after Pa's healing, Yates walked outside and gazed up at the stars. They looked especially close and sparkled as if they wanted to talk to him. A burst of gratitude sprang from his lips as he contemplated God's grand power.

"Thank you, God, for helping my Pa," he said while still looking up. "I sure do appreciate all you've done." Tears clouded his eyes. "I couldn't make myself go up front at church, but I do believe in you and want you in my life. Please help me." He laid his face in his hands while his body shook with sobs.

Someone touched him on the top of his head. He opened his eyes, wiped them with the back of his hand and looked around expecting to see his Pa. No one was there. In bed that night, he thought it over, and decided God sent an angel, or came Himself to let Yates know He heard his prayer.

The next morning the experience was still fresh in his mind, but within days it faded like a vanishing fog. Yates went his way as usual. Soon he forgot about God, but God did not forget about him.

Four

Yates tramped through the underbrush and short Palmetto bushes. Mr. Kingsley led the way. He was a Methodist Preacher and the Kidd's new landlord. Pa and Roby were behind him. Gilbert trailed along beside Yates who stopped from time to time just to look things over and soak up the air in the woods, thankful that Pa was well now and could traipse through the woods with them.

"Look over here, boys," Mr. Kingsley shouted, his voice echoing across the clearing. Yates and Gilbert rushed to catch up and saw a gurgling stream. Sun light glinted on clear water and just below the surface a school of fish wiggled their way down stream.

Pa rubbed his head. "Too bad we don't have a bow and arrow."

"You mean a fish line and sinker, Pa?" Yates asked.

"No, I mean just what I said."

"Pa?". . .

"You boys don't know how to fish with a bow and arrow? I'll bring the stuff and show you next time."

"Down here in Florida," Mr. Kingsley said, "we use palmettos for fishing."

"How in tarnation do you do that?" Gilbert asked.

"Gilbert, don't be using those slang words," Pa corrected.

Mr. Kingsley cut off a frond from a palmetto, stripped the stick of its big green fan and made a sharp point on the end.

"Watch, boys, how to gig for fish." Quick as lightening, he jammed the sharp end of the stick down into the water. He pulled it up and on the end, with the stick run through its middle, flopped a fish.

"Let me try." Excitement danced in Yates' eyes.

Mr. Kingsley handed him the stick. Yates jabbed and jabbed without results.

"Show me again," he pleaded with Mr. Kingsley. They waited for another school of fish. After further instruction and many attempts, with his mouth set just right and determination in his eyes, the stabbing paid off. Yates landed a fish. He let out a whoop bigger than any of his old Indian war whoops.

Pa and the other boys joined him and all working together they soon caught lunch. Pa and Roby cleaned the fish while Yates and Gilbert gathered wood for a fire. Mr. Kingsley brought a cast iron skillet from his wagon along with a pot in which to cook the heart of the palmetto bush. He trimmed and chopped it in pieces, put it in the pot with water from the stream and called it swamp cabbage. The boys soon learned the dish was a Florida specialty eaten with fish.

Roby was getting anxious to get on with their primary mission for this adventure. Ever since he inspected the fifty bee hives around Mr. Kingsley's property, Ma claimed Roby had caught bee fever. That's all he talked about. Finally, Mr. Kinsley promised to take them bee hunting.

That's when they loaded up on his wagon and old Dan, Mr. Kingsley's horse, pulled the wagon to the swampy woods. Old Dan was the only horse the boys ever saw with a beard. His owner said it was from grazing in the pasture so much.

After lunch the team traveled further through the woods on foot. Yates marveled at all the different flowers and bushes they saw. He whistled along with varied birds singing their songs. Suddenly he stopped and pointed. "Look-a there." His mouth dropped open as a long alligator, sunning himself on a log, slid off and glided into the stream. The water rippled around him as he went under. The tip of his head emerged looking like a gray, square box with two bulging eyes sitting on each side of the top.

"Did you ever see the likes of that?" Yates shouted.

"That's common here." Mr. Kingsley answered calmly. He knew all about life in the swamp and enjoyed explaining the different sights and sounds of nature.

Yates loved every minute of their exploring and remarked to Gilbert, "This must be just like heaven."

"Maybe," Gilbert responded.

Finally, Mr. Kingsley stopped, cut another palmetto frond and laid the large fan-shaped leaf on the ground.

"What you doing now?" Yates asked.

"Wait and see," Mr. Kingsley answered.

Yates watched as he drizzled a little bit of honey mixed with water on the frond. They waited. In a few minutes bees were coming and going to the honey. Mr.

Kingsley sprinkled a dusting of flour on their wings to identify which bees returned and to see which direction they went. The process would eventually lead them to the bee tree.

"Well, if that don't beat all." Yates was amazed.

Roby looked like he might just explode with excitement. "This whole bee experience fascinates me to no end," he said to Yates.

They decided after watching the bees come and go that the tree had to be near the river, so they hit the swamp. After trudging about a quarter of a mile they reached the banks of the Alafia, but no tree. Mr. Kingsley said the river flowed some twenty miles and emptied into the Gulf of Mexico. Looking across to the other side of the water they spied a giant cypress.

Mr. Kingsley pointed and shouted, "That's it!"

"How we gonna cross the river?" Roby looked puzzled.

"We can't swim because we need the saw and tools," Mr. Kingsley said. It was too late in the afternoon to carry equipment the long way around.

Pa suggested they go home and get an early start in the morning and come in on the other side of the river.

The next morning Yates helped load Mr. Kingsley's wagon with tubs, saws, axes, and boxes for the bees. They all climbed in with the equipment. Excitement built as they bumped along the path. They had to park the wagon and Old Dan about a quarter of a mile from the bee tree as the growth was too thick to bring it any nearer. They walked into the swamp carrying tools, containers, smokers, and veils.

The tree towered seventy to eighty feet tall and measured about four feet through the trunk. In a knot hole about fifty feet up, coming and going were bees.

Mr. Kingsley and Pa set to sawing with a cross cut saw. When they grew tired the boys took a turn.

"You think we'll ever get this tree cut down?" Roby questioned.

"If we keep at it." Yates answered.

It looked hopeless, but they all cut and sawed until noon. When even Yates thought the job would never end, the tree began to topple.

"Look out, boys!" Pa yelled and the boys scattered. The tree fell to the ground, crashing its way through the smaller trees and underbrush, with a rumble that reverberated through the swamp like a tornado swooping through. The noise quieted quickly, but then another hum began slowly and built up to an almost deafening roar. It sounded like all of creation was alive with swarming, buzzing, mad bees.

The tree split wide open when it fell, exposing a large hollow about eight feet long, full of mad bees and honey comb. Mr. Kingsley knew just what to do. He approached with his smoker and cut out the honey comb filling three wash tubs.

Eventually Mr. Kingsley spotted the queen. She was crushed when the tree fell. He put some bee bread, or honey comb, in his box and bees started going into that container until they completely covered the queen. Mr. Kingsley got all the bees he could in the box, put a screen wire over it and the boys carried everything back to the wagon. They headed home.

On the way, Roby asked Mr. Kingsley what he would do to save the bees since the queen was dead.

"Oh," he said, "they'll make a new queen."

When they arrived at his house they watched as he cut honey comb with broad cells in it and tipped it into the frames. He put the frames in a new hive and put the bees in with the frames.

"How will they make a new queen?" Roby asked.

Mr. Kingsley pointed out to him the broad cells. "Now, you see these cells. They are cells that if left alone will hatch out worker bees, but these bees know that their queen is dead so they go out and get something from the flowers called royal jelly and insert it into their fertile cells. Instead of a worker bee hatching out, a new queen will be developed in that cell. The bees make about seven new queens but the first one that hatches goes around and kills the rest."

A few days later, Mr. Kingsley lifted the cover on the hive and showed Roby and Yates seven cells with a large cut on each one. The new queen had killed all the other prospects before they could overthrow her.

"She must think some things in life are worth fighting for and protecting." Yates said to Roby.

Later, Yates learned that when a queen had outlived her usefulness or was considered defective or an intruder, the worker bees matted into a ball around her and vibrated their muscles so vigorously that it raised the temperature of the queen to a lethal level. It's called, 'balling the queen.' He discussed this new information with Roby, "You reckon humans have a similar way of killing people they don't like?"

Roby frowned "Where did you ever get an idea like that?"

Yates shrugged his shoulders. "Just wondering," he whispered.

Five

1923

The July sun beat down on his head as Yates bent for a watermelon, straightened and laid it in the wagon. He tried to think of the right words to say to Pa. Wiping sweat from his forehead, he blurted out. "I ain't going back to school this fall, Pa."

Pa stopped with a melon in midair and glared at him. "What on earth are you talking about?"

"I'm going to town tomorrow and get a paying job." Yates, now twelve- years-old, had finished the sixth grade that June and thought it was time to help Pa with the finances.

"Don't be foolish, Yates, you need your education."

"I've got enough schooling for now."

"No you don't. That's nonsense." Pa placed the watermelon on the wagon with the rest of the crop, wiped perspiration off the end of his nose.

"Pa, this farm ain't paying off. I'm tired of us working from sun-up till sun-down for next to nothing."

"That's fixing to change. Been figuring . . . starting something new."

"What?" Yates put the last of the fruit on the truck and looked at Pa.

"Building, I can make a fortune on it."

"That'll take forever. You need money now."

"No, Yates. I don't want to hear another word about it." Pa climbed into the wagon, picked up the horse's reins, said "giddy up" and drove off to sell the watermelons.

Yates stomped back to the house muttering, "He's impossible, wouldn't even hear me out."

"Ma," he yelled as the door slammed behind him.

She was in the kitchen stewing squash and frying potatoes for supper. "In here, Yates." Her voice was soft and calm. He knew she would listen to him, and let him talk things over.

He stormed into the kitchen. "Ma, it's time I paid my own way around here. I'm gonna get a job like Roby and Gilbert."

"Where, Yates?"

"Tampa. Pollock's Fish Market needs somebody."

Ma turned to the stove to stir the squash. "We need you on the farm."

Yates felt exasperated. "I'm going tomorrow, Ma."

"Who'll do your chores?" Ma questioned.

"Denson."

"He already has his hands full, son." Ma kept her voice steady.

Denson helped Ma with the laundry on Mondays and Thursdays. There were lots of diapers to wash since Ma gave birth to two more boys, Sam and James.

On those days Denson was up before the sun and out in the back yard pumping fresh water from the well into Ma's big black kettle. After that he built a fire under the pot to boil his baby brother's diapers. Singing to the top of his voice, he scrubbed the soil out on Ma's bumpy washboard.

Next he pumped more water to fill two huge galvanized tubs for rinsing.

It was a big load on Denson, but from the sound of his voice belting out songs, Yates believed that Denson liked to work and wouldn't mind the extra chores.

"He don't wash clothes every day, Ma. He can take up the slack when I'm gone."

"Gone! You mean you're leaving home?" Ma's eyes were pleading. "No, Yates!"

"I have to. I need to be close to my work."

"But, Tampa? That's a big town, too much going on. You need to stay here."

"Aw, Ma! It'll take Pa awhile to make any money in his new building project. Don't you see? I have to help him pay the bills now."

Work was no stranger to Yates. He had always pulled his share of the load and thought he could make it just fine all by himself. He wanted to be like Roby who found a job as soon as they were settled in Florida.

That night, Yates wrapped all his belongings: two shirts, an extra pair of pants, underwear and socks in a brown paper bag. The next morning before daylight, he tiptoed out of the house feeling justified his leaving would give Pa one less mouth to feed.

Yates walked along the edge of the dirt road until the sun came up. Glancing back he saw a vehicle approach and stuck out his thumb. The truck driver slammed on brakes. Yates climbed aboard and they bounced along leaving behind a streak of dust. The driver let Yates off a block from Pollock's Fish Market. His heart pounded in his chest as he approached the two-story building.

Yates entered the store leaving the bright summer sunshine behind. When his eyes adjusted to the dim interior, he found the middle-aged owner.

"Got any work?" Yates voice quivered and he spoke louder than he intended.

Mr. Pollock looked him over. "What can you do?"

"Just about anything. What do you need help with?"

"Cleaning fish."

Yates smiled to boost his own confidence. "You just show me how you want it done and I'll do it."

"Can you drive a truck?"

A cloud crossed Yates face. He had never driven a truck in his life and was surprised that was a requirement. He needed this job and wouldn't go home embarrassed and defeated. *If I can drive a mule, I can handle a truck.* A new philosophy formed in his mind: *if somebody else can do it, so can I.*

He covered his doubt with a smile. "Sure can."

"Then we'll give you a try," Mr. Pollock said. "You can clean fish, wrap them in newspaper, and drive the truck to deliver them to the restaurants."

Yates was relieved, but a little troubled about learning all this so quickly. Then another thought darkened his sun even more. He dropped his head. "You got any place I can sleep?" he mumbled.

"Your Ma know you're leaving home?"

"Yessir, I told her last night."

"Well, in that case." He pointed his finger toward the ceiling. "There's a room upstairs above the market. We could put you a cot up there."

"Whew!" Yates whistled through his teeth.

"Thanks."

"Nobody's been up there in a while, must be covered in dust." Mr. Pollock quickly added. "You'll have to clean it."

"I'd be glad to do that, sir." *Boy! That takes a load off my mind. Now I gotta learn to drive that truck before he finds out I don't really know how.* He had watched Pa and Roby drive. When the time came, he would do what they did.

"By the way boy, what's your name?"

"Oh, 'scuse me, Mr. Pollock, sir, I forgot to introduce myself. My name is Kidd, Yates Warren Kidd." He grinned and stuck out his hand.

Mr. Pollock took it and looked at Yates hard. "You got yourself a job, Kidd, but I expect you to give me a good day's work."

"Yessir, I will. You can count on that." He didn't bat an eyelid but looked Mr. Pollock straight in the eyes and said, "I ain't afraid of work."

The old brown boards squeaked as Yates trudged up the narrow stairs to the small room above the market. With each step the heat increased. Once he arrived at the top perspiration made wet spots on his shirt under his arms. The stifling room was bare except for a rickety old chair which sat on one side with a little scratched table beside it.

He slung his bag of clothes on the chair and looked around. Spider webs filled the corners and drab unpainted board walls surrounded the room. Two dingy windows were still clear enough that the sun shone through, and made a big checked pattern on the floor. To Yates the bright spots said, *Welcome Home.* He had a place of his own.

Flinging open the windows Yates raised his arms and let the breeze blow on the damp places of his shirt. Once cool he found a broom and gave the room a good sweeping, killing the spiders that ran when he brushed down their webs. Mrs. Pollock heated a bucket of water on her wood stove. Yates toted the hot, soapy liquid upstairs, and mopped the room like it was Ma's kitchen floor.

Good to his word, when the floor dried Mr. Pollock climbed the stairs to help Yates set up the cot. Mrs. Pollock followed with clean sheets made from feed sacks. She gave Yates a pillow, a clean towel, a washcloth and small bar of Ivory soap, then told him where to find a washbasin, a clean bucket and a dipper. He collected them, scooted out to the pump, filled the bucket with drinking water, toted it up the stairs, and set it on the table.

After completing that task he decided to visit the Pollock's apartment connected to the fish market. Yates went downstairs and knocked. In a few seconds, Mrs. Pollock swung the door open.

He swallowed and found the courage to speak, "I just wanted to say thanks for fixing my bed and giving me a pillow and stuff."

"You're welcome."

Her friendly face and cheerful voice helped ease Yates shyness. Still he looked down at his feet. "Could I pay you back and fetch a bucket of water for ya."

"Why, that would be real nice, Yates."

"I don't mind." Yates lifted his head and looked at her. "I'm used to helping Ma." He grabbed the bucket and rushed out to the pump.

When it was dark, Yates went upstairs and lay down on his new bed. He thought about Ma and the little ones at home. Tears surfaced, but he swallowed them back to keep from bawling like a baby. He wondered how upset Pa was to find out he had gone. He believed Pa would change his tune when he took money home to help feed the family. The thought made him feel a little better.

Lying there in the dark, Yates remembered Roby and the day his older brother scouted the countryside looking for work. At sundown, Roby was about to give up, when he stumbled onto an old farm house built in an orange grove. The owner and his wife sat on the porch tuckered out after a hard day's work. The man hired Roby on the spot to spread fertilizer around the orange trees, which was a two week job and didn't pay much.

The old couple was childless and took to Roby like a duck to water. They begged him to move in with them after the two weeks were over. They said he could help with chores and they would feed him and give him a little money. He ended up staying with them through the week and going home for Saturdays and Sundays. That left more food on the table at home and gave Roby a couple of dollars to bring Pa for the family.

Yates had already made up his mind to pattern after Roby. Lying there on the cot he decided he wouldn't give all the money to Pa though. He'd remember Ma, too, and take her something special to eat.

Yates felt grateful for his new job, his room and the chance to help his family. His loneliness faded as he drifted off to sleep.

The next morning, sun streamed into the window

and woke Yates in time to wash up and dress before Mrs. Pollock called him down to breakfast. The smell of bacon frying and coffee perking greeted him. He came down the stairs feeling more and more at home. Mrs. Pollock smiled as she passed him one of her fluffy homemade biscuits.

"Did you sleep well, Yates?" Her soft voice sounded a little bit like his Ma's.

"Yes Ma'am," he said taking the biscuit.

"You look mighty young," she continued. "Bet you miss your Ma."

"Yes Ma'am. But I'm twelve, that's old, enough . . ."

Mrs. Pollock missed her own sons who were grown and gone from home. She suspected this boy would claim a spot beside them in her maternal affections. Already, she felt like a mother hen about to take a new chick under her protective wing.

Mr. Pollock ate like he was going to a fire. Yates tried to keep up and make polite conversation with Mrs. Pollock at the same time. Mr. Pollock got ahead of him and was ready to start work way before Yates finished his eggs and grits. Finally, he crammed the last of the biscuit in his mouth. "I'm coming, sir," he said and ran after him.

"We ain't got all day, Kidd. Got fish to clean."

"Yessir,"

The stale odor of old fish greeted them as Mr. Pollock swung open the door to the market. He showed Yates around the shop. A long table stood in the middle of the room. The center was covered with nicks and scratches where the sharp filet knives dug into the wooden top. On one end of the slab sat a lopsided stack of newspapers. Here and there, fish scales curled on the floor. Yates grabbed a broom, swept them onto a piece of the folded paper, and dumped them in the smelly trash barrel where the fish guts went.

Mr. Pollock grinned and slapped Yates on the shoulder. "You gonna do all right, Kidd."

Yates smiled back. He heard the slow clomping of a horse outside. The animal pulled an ice wagon over to the doorway and neighed as his driver reined him in and tied him to a hitching post.

"Go out and help the iceman, Kidd." Mr. Pollock's eyes twinkled when he added, "Think you can lift those heavy pieces?"

"Sure I can," Yates shot back over his shoulder.

The blocks of ice weighed 50 pounds each, but Yates forked them up with the giant ice tongs as if they were firewood. They were heavy, but he had a strong back and legs that could handle it. With a long ice pick, he chipped the big chunks into small pieces and put it in the cooler ready for the fish to arrive. Soon the fishermen came with their night catch of mullet.

Mr. Pollock went to work. His hands flew as he scaled the fish and gutted them with a few short moves. "Knife's gotta be sharp, that's important."

"Yessir." In no time, Yates was cleaning and filleting fish like a pro. A portion of them went on ice for customers who came into the market. Mr. Pollock showed Yates how to wrap the rest just right in newspaper, and the next thing they knew it was time to take them to the restaurants on the route.

Mr. Pollock called his wife to come and watch the

store while they left to deliver the fish.

"I'll drive the first two or three days. Show you where to go." Mr. Pollock jangled the truck keys.

Yates nodded and breathed a sigh of relief. This gave him a chance to watch and fix in his mind exactly how to shift the gears. As they delivered fish to all the restaurants on the list, Yates watched every move Mr. Pollock made and memorized the exact steps to driving a truck. In his mind, he drew a map of directions to the locations.

The fourth day after they cleaned and wrapped the fish, Mr. Pollock threw his keys to Yates. "Think you can handle it today, Kidd?"

"Sure can." He caught the keys and loaded the fish. Showtime! He swung up into the truck, put the key in the ignition and turned it, glad the truck had one of those new electric starters and not the old fashion hand crank. He tried to act like he had done this plenty of times. *Now let's see. Put both feet on the pedals, Put the clutch in – shift the gears, let the clutch out, and press the gas.* He went step by step. The truck gave a lurch and died. *Oh, No!* Yates glanced out the window and caught Mr. Pollock's grin. "Thought you could drive, boy."

"I can." Yates set his jaw firmly.

"Let the clutch out easy, and step on the gas gently," Mr. Pollock said.

"Yessir." Yates got it that time and away he went chug-a-lugging along thinking, *I can drive!* There was only one problem. Half grown and too short for his feet to reach the pedals, he came off the seat each time he put on brakes to stop the truck. It seemed dangerous and exciting to him.

He knew his Pa would never stand for that kind of a risk and it made him feel daring and brave. He overlooked the fact that he could have an accident, and thought instead that he was helping Mr. Pollock, Pa and himself.

At the end of the week when Mr. Pollock paid his five dollar wage, Yates went to the store and bought Ma a beef roast, a loaf of white bread, six lemons, a five pound bag of sugar and a basket of peaches. His bill was $1.57, but Ma was worth it.

He caught a ride out to the farm and handed Pa two dollars.

Pa's eyes glistened. "Thank you, son. This'll come in mighty good this week." He put the money in his pocket and Yates knew it would buy enough groceries to give them several good meals.

Ma's eyes lit up when she peered into the sack from the store. "Why, Yates! You bought my favorite foods. I'm going to make a big pitcher of lemonade right now."

All the children gathered around Yates begging for a slice of the store bought bread. They laughed and talked like Yates was their hero. It gave him a good warm feeling and made him think he was grown.

When he got back to his room at the fish market and knew he had fulfilled his duty to help Ma and Pa he decided to buy something for himself. Something he had craved since the move to Florida. He was on his own now and nobody was there to tell him he couldn't. The next day he went to the store and bought himself a pack of cigarettes.

* * *

Within weeks after Yates left home, Pa began working to

develop one of the dreams that he had figured on for years: his building project. From then on, when he drove the wagon to Tampa with a load of watermelons or cucumbers, he scouted the area for land and finally found a plot in an up and coming area called Oak Park. Pa's business sense told him that the city was spreading out and soon the area would need more homes. The community already had a school and a scattering of houses. Pa planned to build nice comfortable homes that the average worker could afford.

All of Pa's figuring in the past prepared him for this day. He spent hours writing plans for a housing subdivision. When they were completed, he delivered them to an architect to draw up the blueprints. Excitement built with each step and so did doubt. Could he undertake such a large project? His health was fine now and his sons young and strong. With their help he believed the plan would work. Confidence began to build along with the ideas.

Finally, one day, with the proposal rolled up and stuck under his arm, Pa gathered his courage and walked into a bank.

He watched the clock on the wall until the time arrived for Pa's talk with the banker. With shaking hands, he unrolled the designs, and laid them out on the desk.

"I've found a plot of land off of Columbus Drive in East Tampa," he began, his voice quivering. "It's an ideal spot for a subdivision. Here are the blueprints for the houses I intend to build. This area is growing, with new families moving in every day. They need housing. I can provide it at a reasonable price."

"Wait a minute, Mr. . . Err, what was your name again?"

"Neuby Kidd."

"Mr. Kidd, this is an enormous project. We don't just loan money at a whim. We need collateral. What do you own?"

"Well, I don't rightly own anything at the present."

"Come back when you have something to offer. Good day, sir." The banker shook Pa's hand and turned to leave.

"Wait just a minute. You haven't seen my figures yet."

"Figures don't mean anything. We need collateral. Banks don't take risks."

"Sir, with all due respect, please hear me out. I can show you in black and white that what I plan to do is not a risk.

Pa pulled out his pad and pencil. "See here is the cost of materials for this particular house." Pa turned the page on his pad; and how much I'll need to pay the workers." He turned another page "Here's the price the house would sell for." Pa turned one more page. "This, sir, is the profit I can make and still give the buyer a good deal."

The banker scratched his head. "I can see, Mr. Kidd, that you have done your homework. It looks good on paper but that doesn't mean it would work."

"Wouldn't work? Sir, it's all right here in the figures. I have priced everything right down to the last penny."

"I can't just hand out money, Mr. Kidd, because you have figures on paper. You need more. I'm sorry."

Pa gathered up his papers and left. He opened the

door and blinked in the bright sunlight. His throat felt constricted. He remembered passing a new bank down the road. He went there, told the banker he had four sons to help with the building and he owned a horse and buggy. The banker hardly batted an eye when he drew up the papers. Pa signed on the dotted line for enough money to build the first house.

Pa was in business.

He hired a skeleton crew and the work began. Cut out to be a boss, Pa treated the men with dignity and they gave him a good day's work for top wages. Roby and Gilbert worked beside Pa. Yates helped out after work hours at the Fish Market and on Saturdays. Denson was big enough to tote water and boards after school.

The first house sold quickly. Pa made enough for the next house and saved some. He continued to build and sell until he saved enough money to build a house for his family.

Moving day was a happy time. Pa was glad to be close to his job and Ma thrilled that the school was right down the street. Now she stood outside in the dew dampened mornings and watched Denson, Virgie and Mary swing their lunch pails as they walked to school together. Baby James cooed and nestled in her arms in the early morning sun while tottering Sam hung on to her skirt-tail, turning loose long enough to wave at his departing brother and two sisters.

Ma loved living in town and planted colorful Zinnias around her door. It was nice to be close enough that Yates could visit often. Ma laughed more and more since life had taken a better turn for the Kidd family.

Six

1927

One night shortly after Yates' sixteenth birthday, he slicked his hair back with the new wonder Brylcream and coaxed a wave in the top. Then he dashed on Aqua Velva shaving lotion. He wanted to look and smell just right that evening for Merle. Yates thought she was a cute little tomato and he had asked her to go on a double date. Guy Planter, a friend of Yates, asked his girl, and the foursome planned to go to a moving picture show.

They picked the girls up at six-thirty. Yates thought Merle was a real eyeful as he walked her to Guy's new roadster. When the boys escorted the girls into the theater, the smell of hot buttered popcorn lured them. While they bought a bag, Roby and Gilbert came through the door with their girlfriends in tow. The eight teens took up an entire row.

Halfway through the movie Yates curled his arm around Merle's shoulder. She didn't protest his advances and he spent the rest of the show imagining what she might let him do later. He'd heard about fast girls and wondered if she was that kind. He licked the salt off of his lips in anticipation.

After the movie, they headed home. In the one-seat

roadster squeezed in tight beside Merle, Yates enjoying the ride, plotted his next move, but the swift little car arrived at her house far too soon to suit him. Disappointed, he walked her to the door and reached to kiss her. Just as their lips met her father opened the door. Yates jumped and dashed back to the car.

He liked Merle, but didn't plan on being saddled with any girl for the rest of his life. He just wanted a little fun and see how far she might let him go.

Guy deposited his girl on her doorstep. He had better luck than Yates and planted a kiss on her lips. Smiling, he got in the car and put it in gear. "Next time I'll really kiss her a good one."

Yates laughed. "Yeah, me too. Merle's Daddy messed it up for me."

"You gotta plan ahead," Guy advised.

The boys turned a corner and spotted Roby and Gilbert crossing the street. Guy screeched to a halt and asked if they wanted to go for a ride in his new roadster.

Gilbert nodded. Yates opened the door and got out.

Roby sized up the car. "We can't all fit in there."

"Yeah, we can." Yates said. "Get in Roby. You can sit in the middle."

Gilbert crawled in next on the passenger side. That left no place for Yates but on Gilbert's lap. He folded himself in and somehow managed to close the door. The four boys were packed in that little car like sardines. They rode a ways laughing and talking.   "Where we going?" Roby sounded like he could hardly breathe crowded in on both sides.

"I hope it's not far or Yates will have me squashed

to death." Gilbert piped up. "Ease up a little bit, Hoot. Your bones are going right through me."

Yates tried to adjust himself but there wasn't room for moving. "Where *are* we going, Guy?"

"There's a Klan meeting out in the woods tonight. Thought we'd go hide out a while and see what they do."

Roby's face looked strained in the little bit of light from the dash. "I don't think we need to go spying on the Klan. That'll come to no good."

"It'll be all right Roby. Me and Yates have already been out there once."

Yates squirmed on his brother's lap.

"Yates went?" Even in the dark, they all felt the tension. "You went, Yates?"

"Aw, lay off Roby. No need to get in a lather." Guy turned his head toward him. "You ought a go see for yourself. It's a sight. All of 'em in them long robes with holes cut where they can peek out."

"I don't want to see them. Pa's against it and I've heard some talk myself about beatings and killings."

"Naw, you're all wet on that. My Daddy said they believe in good things and are jest trying to get people to keep the law. Me and Yates have been looking into it and we might join 'em, soon as we get old enough."

Yates swallowed hard wishing Guy had kept his mouth shut. He didn't want Roby to know.

"I don't see no harm in going to find out what they believe." Gilbert squirmed under the weight of Yates' body. "Anything to get Yates off my lap."

Yates gave a nervous laugh, shifted his position and changed the subject from the Klan. "Open this baby up and see how fast it'll run."

"Oh, it'll run all right." Guy stomped the gas pedal, Yates jerked back against Gilbert's chest as the car lurched and shot forward. He let out a whoop you could have heard to Georgia. Even Roby laughed.

"This is what you call *joy riding,*" Yates said and turned his head to watch the road fly by, excitement flowing through his veins.

They rounded a wide sweeping curve and suddenly headlights blinded them.

Raw fear jolted each of the boys.

Guy slammed on brakes. They squalled and he let up a bit to gain control.

"He's on our side of the road!" Yates yelled.

"Heading straight for us!" Guy jammed the brakes again and yanked the steering wheel hard to the right. They bounced. The car felt crazy . . . out of control. The nose of the car went down an embankment, the tail flipping over and over. Yates head hit hard. He heard glass breaking. He couldn't constrain his flailing arms and legs as he sailed through the air. The smell of dirt went up his nose when he hit the ground. A hot searing pain that felt like fire shot through his right hip.

* * *

Ma heard the mournful sound of a siren wailing in the night and sat up in bed, her heart pounding. *That's one of my boys!* "Oh, God, help my sons."

She prayed until she felt a sense of relief. Lying back on her pillow she dozed off and on, dreaming of a smashed car. . . faces crowded around . . . ambulances that came and went. She stood at a distance and wrung her hands crying out for God to take care of her boys.

Waking with a start, she heard a rap on the door and shook Pa lying beside her. "Neuby, wake up! Somebody's at the door."

With his eyes half opened, Pa sat up and reached for his trousers. Pulling them on, he said softly, "Coming."

Ma donned her bathrobe and tiptoed behind him. "I just know something has happened to one of the boys," she whispered.

Pa unlatched the door and swung it open to find a police officer.

"Sorry to disturb you this late," he said. "Are you Mr. Kidd?"

"Yes."

"Do you have a son named Yates?" Pa nodded and Ma hid behind him biting her bottom lip.

"Oh God, what's happened," she breathed.

"There's been an accident. Yates is at Tampa Municipal Hospital. He's hurt pretty bad."

They dressed quickly and went to the hospital, Ma praying all the way.

* * *

Hours passed before Yates emerged from the darkness to the smell of ether and alcohol. He opened his eyes in a hospital bed. Pain, like he had never felt before, radiated from his right hip. Ma sat beside him, holding his hand in both of hers. Tears wet her cheeks.

"Oh, Yates," she smiled faintly, "You're awake. Thank God."

"What's wrong, Ma?"

"You were in a bad accident."

It all came flooding back: the car lights, Guy's vehicle tumbling from end to end, the crashing windshield, being propelled through the air and finally the pain – the hot pain that he still felt.

This was Yates' third wreck since leaving home four years ago. In each crash, the car was either smashed or turned upside down. He was not behind the wheel in any of the accidents and still called himself a safe driver.

"Where is Roby and Gilbert, Ma?"

Roby stepped up, "Right here, Hoot."

"You ain't hurt, Roby?"

"No, but Gilbert skinned his legs. He's sitting over there in a chair."

Yates nodded slightly and a weak smile crossed his lips before he remembered. "What about Guy?"

"Didn't get a scratch on him," Roby said. "But it sure messed up that little roadster of his. Nobody'll ride in it for a while."

Gilbert hobbled over to the bed, his legs bandaged. "The driver in the other car was drunk, Yates. Hit a tree. Killed him."

Ma sobbed and laid her head face down on the bed then she raised it with tears streaming down her face. "You could have all been killed. It was only God that protected you boys." She put her head down again and sobbed uncontrollably.

Yates felt his eyes water and his hand shook as he stroked Ma's head.

When her crying lessened, she said, "I heard the siren in the night, Yates, and knew that one of my boys was hurt. I've been praying for you ever since the policeman came to the door."

"Thanks, Ma."

Pa and a man in a white coat walked into the room. The man held a wooden contraption with screws at the top and bottom. It was the length of Yates' leg.

Pa stepped up to the bed. "You can be thankful you're alive, son. You boys must have been going too fast in that little car." He turned to the man beside him. "This here is Doctor Jones. Gonna fix your broken hip."

The man in the white coat moved to the side of the bed and told Yates that he was not going to put his leg in a cast, instead, he had something new that would do a better job. Then he showed Yates the brown wooden device and explained that he intended to put it on Yates' leg and hip. Every morning and evening he would turn the screws that caused the mechanism to pull the bones in place while nature took its course and knitted them back together.

"Hope you know what you're doing, Doc." Yates looked at him suspiciously. It sounded right but something in his gut told him different.

Pa cleared his throat. "Now, Yates, I think you better cooperate with the Doctor here. He's studied all this out."

Yates turned his head away; tears ran out the corners of his eyes. "My hip hurts so bad, Pa," he whispered.

"I know, son, but the doctor is here to help."

Something about it wasn't right to Yates, but he didn't want to argue with Pa.

Every day as he laid in the hospital bed the doctor came in the room and turned the screws. The action caused excruciating pain that never left.

"I don't think this thing is working Doc," he told him often.

"Sure it is," the doctor answered.

Yates' legs had always been strong. He wondered what he would do if his hip didn't heal. Maybe he wouldn't be able to walk.

Three months later, Doctor Jones took the contraption off and told Yates that his hip had mended and he wanted him to move around. When he helped Yates off the bed his legs buckled. The pain was awful.

"This hip ain't right, Doc." Yates frowned.

"You haven't walked in a while," he said. "What you need now is exercise. I want you to walk a mile each day."

"You don't mean that."

"Yes, I do."

"It hurts too bad to walk."

"That is the only way to make the pain go away."

"I want to do what you say, Doc, but it just don't seem right."

"It's the only way." He turned, walked a few steps, looked back at Yates and said, "Walk." He nodded and left the room.

Day after day, it was sheer torture as Yates put one foot in front of the other, obeyed Doctor Jones and walked. He told himself *I'm a man now; I can handle a little pain.*

He set a goal to get from one light pole to the next. When he reached a pole, he sat on the ground and cried. Then he got up and walked to the next one, determined to help him-self get better.

After two weeks of this routine, Yates went back to work at the fish market. The pain was worse than ever. The following day he didn't wake up for work. The clock was striking two in the afternoon when Mr. Pollack bounded up the stairs to see why he had not come down to his job. He banged on the door. "Kidd, you there?" When there was no response, he burst the door open and found Yates unconscious. Sirens blared as the ambulance rushed him back to the hospital.

In the emergency room doctors took new x-rays that revealed a problem with the wooden contraption. Each time Doctor Jones turned the screws, instead of aligning the bones, as it was designed to do, it pulled them too far apart. Yates still had a broken hip.

In a few days Doctor Jones left town.

The hospital staff called in a new doctor from a golf game. Yates knew the minute Doctor Grange bent to examine his hip that he had done more than hit a golf ball. His breath reeked of alcohol and he slurred his words. Pa didn't seem to notice and, before Yates could tell anyone, they whisked him off to surgery. His last thoughts before the anesthesia took effect were: *the first doctor failed and now I lay helpless in the hands of one who got himself a snoot full.* Yates wondered if the doctor could see straight enough to perform surgery.

The drunken doctor set Yates' hipbone and began to wrap him in white gauze to make a plaster cast. He started at one ankle and wrapped each leg separately then continued across his hips, stomach and chest binding his arms to his body. When he had finished the cast he wedged a two by four between Yates' legs. There he lay, like a mummy, with his legs spread apart by the board. He stared up at the ceiling, counting cracks in it, unable to move anything but his head, hands and toes. He nearly went stir crazy in that uncomfortable position.

One day soon after the surgery, everything took on a golden hue. "Hey, Nurse," Yates said, "You look golden and glowing."

"Quit flirting with me, Yates." She smiled and went about her duties with other patients.

"Everything looks that way," Yates said, but she was already gone. He looked at the shimmering window beside his bed, but it faded away. No, there it was again – sparkling. His breath came in shallow gasps. He felt a sensation of leaving his body – floating in space. The whole room glistened, faded and returned as Yates lapsed in and out of consciousness.

Another nurse passed the bed, looked at him and ran out of the room. In a few moments she was back with a doctor. He cut a hole in the cast at the middle. Yates' stomach puffed out through the hole like a balloon and he drew a long deep breath.

"You had a close call, Kidd," the doctor said. "Already turned blue. A few more seconds and you would have been gone."

The nurse adjusted his pillow and bent to his ear. "Somebody upstairs must be looking out for you."

"Yeah," he whispered back. But in his heart he questioned if God was looking out for him. If so where was God when the car hit them and why was he laying there broken up with his body immovable? Yet he knew something spared his life – twice.

Nine long months Yates lay in the body cast looking up. He knew every detail of that stucco ceiling and the walls around him. There were patterns and faces in the plaster. He imagined who they were and made up stories about them to tell his two little sisters when they came for a visit.

Those were the brightest spots during his long time of confinement, the days that Pa and Ma brought Virgie and Mary to see him. They had grown into beautiful girls of ten and eight. Each time they peeked around the door and said "Hey, Yates," in their southern drawl, he smiled.

After they left, Yates lay there and thought about their future. He devised speeches to give them when they were older. Before they reached the teenage years he planned to warn them about boys and how they tried to take advantage of pretty girls like them.

Doctor Granger came to check on Yates the first two weeks. After that, Doctor Hance replaced him in the daily rounds.

The time finally arrived when Dr. Hance would cut off the cast. To Yates, that day felt better than Christmas. Outside the sun shone brightly and streamed through the window of his room bringing in a cheerful light. He tingled with excitement. When he thought about walking again, he felt like he might explode with joy.

Pa and Ma came for the momentous occasion and stood by the bed smiling and talking. Ma's eyes twinkled like she was as happy as Yates. And Pa spoke to him about coming back home for a few days to get his strength back. Yates agreed.

It took a while for the doctor to saw the cast. When

he pulled the last bit away, Yates felt air hit his body and he breathed a sigh of relief. He began to rub his chest, arms and legs. They ached and he could barely move them. But they did move. A broad smile stretched across his face. "Free as a bird." He said.

Doctor Hance took him by the hand and pulled him to a sitting position. When Yates gained his balance the doctor helped him off the bed. For the first time in nine months, Yates' feet touched the floor. A thousand needles began in the soles of his feet and moved up his legs. That was not surprising. He expected discomfort after not walking all those months. He understood that the feeling in his limbs would return to normal when the blood flow improved. But, something just didn't feel right. When he took the first step his right foot went down like he had stepped into a hole. He tried the left one and it brought him back up.

Yates broke out in a cold sweat. "What's wrong here, Doc?"

The doctor's eyes grew wide. "Get back on the bed, Kidd." He left the room quickly and returned in a few minutes with a tape measure. After telling Yates to lie flat he measured both legs. When he raised his head all the color had drained from his face. "Your hip didn't heal properly." He said and shook his head in disbelief. "Your right leg is three inches shorter than your left one."

Yates gaped and stared.

Ma gasped, "No!"

"How did this happen, Doctor?" Lines etched across Pa's forehead.

"I'm not sure." Doctor Hance scratched the back of

his head. "I didn't perform the surgery."

"I'll tell you how it happened," Yates voice trembled. "That doctor was drunk when he operated on me."

"Drunk!" Pa's voice rose. "You should 'a said something."

"Didn't have a chance." Yates clamped his jaw.

"It's too late now to place blame." Ma's voice was gentle, her eyes dark. She shook her head and mumbled, "Three inches shorter. I can't believe it."

"I don't understand this." Pa's eyes begged for help. "Can you fix it, Doctor Hance?"

The doctor slowly shook his head. "I can't. We'll have to inquire. There may be a doctor up North. . ."

Pa's eyebrows shot up. "You mean there's not a doctor in Florida that can do it?"

"I'm not sure Mr. Kidd. We'll check."

"Doctors," Pa grunted. "Drunk and operating on my boy." He scratched his head. "That first doctor didn't know what he was doing either . . . with that contraption." Agitation sounded in Pa's voice as it grew loud.

"I know this is hard on all of you, Mr. Kidd, but try to keep your voice down," Doctor Hance said. "No need to disturb the other patients."

"The other patients! What about my son? This hospital has ruined him." Pa's voice cracked.

"Now, Mr. Kidd, let's not blame the hospital for the mistakes of two doctors."

"We just want our son's leg fixed," Ma whispered and put her hands over her face.

Doctor Hance patted Ma's shoulder. "I'm sorry

Mrs. Kidd; I don't know what else to tell you."

"Something's got to be done. I'm going to the main office. . . Talk to somebody about fixing this leg." Pa left the room with his head down.

The doctor's words played over and over in Yates head, *right leg three inches shorter.* He bent his arm to cover his eyes. The nurses' words echoed in his ears, somebody's *looking out for you.* He squeezed his eyes shut and wondered where was God now? The victory of the day was gone, vanished as though someone put a shield over the sun – permanently.

Yates knew, unless Pa got him help, he would limp as long as he lived.

After a long time, Pa returned to the room with papers in his hand. He shoved them at Ma. "They won't tell me anybody that can help Yates. . . Don't even know if his leg can be fixed." Pa shook his head and took a deep breath letting it out slowly. "The hospital has already fired those two doctors, Josie; they won't do anything else to make this right. They told me that my only recourse is to sue the doctors."

Ma's eyes opened wide. "Go to court?"

"Yes."

"What'd you tell them?" Ma asked.

"Said I'd let them know in a day or two." Pa breathed a long sigh. "They're out to get those two doctors, stop them from practicing medicine. Want me to help." He looked out the window and said half to himself. "It seems like a terrible thing to take away a man's work after all those years of study." He shook his head and sighed again. "I don't know if I can do that."

Yates raised his head. "They messed up my leg, Pa."

"I know son, but do you think they did it on purpose? They're not God, you know- only men. Men make mistakes.

"But, Pa . . ." Yates didn't understand the change in Pa's attitude. How could he take up for the men who had made him a cripple? Rage rose in him. Suddenly he wanted to shake Pa until his teeth rattled. He dropped back on the pillow.

How he wanted to hit the drunk who ruined his leg. No, he wanted to beat him to a bloody pulp. And if he could get his hands on the man who forced him to walk on a broken hip, he'd break both of his legs.

Instead, Yates turned his head toward the wall and squeezed his hands into fists until his nails dug into the skin.

* * *

That night Pa tossed and turned in his bed, tormented with the decision before him. Should he take the doctors to court and put them out of work permanently? If he won, he could get money and look for a better doctor up north to help Yates. But, was there a better doctor out there? Two had already tried and made a mess. It was hard to trust anybody now. Maybe it wasn't their fault. Maybe no one else could have done better. If somebody else tried to fix it they might make it worse. At least he could walk, even if he did limp. Another doctor might ruin it; then Yates couldn't walk at all.

Maybe he should just trust God to heal Yates like He had healed him and forget about suing the doctors.

Finally he got up and found his Bible. It fell open at I Corinthians 6:7. *There is a fault among you,* he read, *because you go to the law one with another. Why do you not rather take wrong?* It went on to say that people were defrauding their brother by taking them to court.

The words rang out all night in Pa's mind. Time and again he heard *don't take your brother to court.* Then a new tune started, *Do unto others as you would have them do unto you.* Before daybreak, he made his decision.

When the sun came up, Pa went back to the hospital. Two men came to Yates' room for the signed papers. Pa told them that he couldn't do it.

"Mr. Kidd, you could sue and get money to go up North and try to find a specialist."

"I was almost convinced of that, but I just can't do it." Pa shook his head.

The man looked down then back at Pa. "I don't understand."

"I don't fully either. I just know that I wouldn't want someone taking away my livelihood over a mistake and the Bible says not to take your brother to court."

The man shook his head. "Mr. Kidd, you could help us stop these doctors. Think about it."

"I thought about it all night."

He took a deep breath. "If you change your mind I'll be in my office."

Yates watched him walk out the door knowing Pa would never change his mind. He breathed a long sigh. It didn't make any sense. How could Pa think like that? Those doctors's needed to be stopped from their blunders and they were not his brothers. They were his enemies who ruined him. Pa was the only one with the authority to sue and get his leg fixed. He refused because God didn't want him to? Yates wondered what kind of a God would do that.

He choked back his anger along with his tears and buried them out of sight. He would never show how he really felt toward either of them – Pa or God.

Seven

Yates struggled with the limp. He practiced walking, but no matter how hard he tried, his body went up and down, side to side with each step.

Whenever he was in a crowd and heard a person snicker he thought they laughed at him and his crooked walk. Every now and then he heard someone whisper the word, *cripple.* He knew they were talking about him behind his back.

Embarrassment, sadness and irritation rotated in his emotions. Gone was his even temperament. He fought to regain control of these feelings but believed his life was ruined. Nightmares of the fateful accident that left him lame tormented his sleep. Anger that began in the hospital toward Pa grew into a monster. He tried to choke it back, swallow it and hide it behind a smile. It grew harder to gulp down and nearly impossible to smile.

During the long months that Yates was in the hospital he didn't see much of Gilbert. He visited a few times and at first seemed like himself, but later he acted different – distant. The brothers had always been close and Yates wondered what was wrong.

One day, after Yates went home with Ma and Pa, Gilbert came by and went straight to the back yard. Yates followed and walked up behind him as Gilbert hid something in his jacket pocket.

"What's that?"

Gilbert walked away. "None of your business."

Yates hobbled after him, grabbed his arm and swung him around. "Don't you ignore me," Yates said through clenched teeth. He reached in Gilbert's coat and drew out a bottle. "Where'd you get this?"

"I said, 'It's none of your business.'"

The brothers stood glaring at each other for what seemed like eternity. Yates broke the stare by jerking the lid off the bottle. He looked at the amber liquid, swished it around inside and took a long swig. When he pulled the bottle away from his lips, he coughed and spewed half of it on the ground. "That stuff tastes awful."

"It gets better after a while."

As the booze hit Yates stomach he felt warmth flow through his body. He turned the bottle up again and this time he swallowed the whole gulp. In a few minutes his leg didn't seem so important.

He learned that Gilbert always had a pint stashed. If Yates felt insecure he could depend on Gilbert for a shot.

When Yates went back to work cleaning fish he had to stand on the ball of his right foot to balance his body. It tired him and he shifted the weight from leg to leg. If he put his right foot down his left leg bent at the knee. Soon that was uncomfortable and he shifted back to the ball of his foot. After awhile both hips hurt and he longed to sit and rest them. He knew that wouldn't be fair to Mr. Pollock, he had promised to give him a full day's work.

He was good at covering up his discomfort and

made up his mind that he would never complain. At the same time he was learning his limitations. He knew there was nothing to do but find another job, one where he could sit more. The owner of the lumber yard where Pa bought his building materials hired Yates to drive a truck. He knew Yates as a hard worker in spite of his handicap. As a bonus his friend E. T. Fox was a co-worker.

Yates was relieved yet torn by his love and loyalty to his old job. He hated to leave the fish market with all its customers. He enjoyed seeing them and the exchange of talk. And especially, he hated to leave Mr. and Mrs. Pollock who had become his second family. Telling them good-by was worse than surgery, but there was nothing else he could do.

They offered to let him keep the room upstairs but it didn't seem fair to them. They might need it for another employee. Beside it took him too long now, to climb the stairs. Before the accident he could bound up the stairs two at the time. Now he had to stop on each one and drag his short leg up.

He cleaned out his belongings and moved back home for good with Pa and Ma. When he brought in his things, Ma laughed and wiped tears from her eyes at the same time. She hugged him over and over and cooked his favorite dishes.

Pa hugged him too but Yates felt himself stiffen at his touch. Pa was kind to him and never had a cross word. He still woke up singing. Yet, Yates kept a distance between them.

At first he felt strange to be surrounded by baby brothers he barely knew, but nice to get to know them better. Sam and James soon looked up to their big brother. Yates catered to them bringing them treats and looking out for their safety.

On the new job he had to help load the truck which was better than standing in one spot like he did at the fish market. And he only stopped once to deliver the materials, a far less painful task than when he crawled in and out of the truck at many restaurants.

When Yates walked he seldom put his right heal down. The effort made his whole body bend to the side and his gait too uneven. Putting all of his weight on the ball of that foot made it sore. Walking became harder and harder. He worried that soon he wouldn't be able to move around at all. It scared him and he turned again to Gilbert's bottle.

Finally, he bought a pint of his own. Regardless of how surly it made Gilbert, Yates determined the booze would not affect him like that. He would control it; take it like medicine to get through this bad time. When he got used to his short leg and no longer needed it, he'd quit.

* * *

When some semblance of a normal life returned, one night Yates and Guy rode out to the dense woods where the Klan met, supposedly a *secret* meeting place, but Klan recruiters whispered its whereabouts.

They watched and listened from the bushes as men in white robes streamed into the clearing from every direction. The King Gleagle opened by shouting K I G Y.

Yates and Guy exchanged looks, wondering what in the world he meant. Later they learned the secret code meant *Klansmen, I Greet You.*

The hooded men chanted their creed. It went

something like this:

> *We are the White Knights of the Ku Klux Klan, members of an invisible empire. A Christian, fraternal and benevolent organization to protect the weak, the innocent, and the defenseless from the indignities, wrongs and outrages of the lawless, the violent, and the brutal; To relieve the injured and oppressed; To succor the suffering and unfortunate, and especially the widows and orphans.*

To help the weak, innocent, widows and orphans sounded like something from the Bible Yates heard at the Tabernacle. That appealed to Him. He thought it was the type of thing that Ma raised him to do. He knew she would be proud of him if he joined and helped these men.

When he and Guy came out of the bushes one of the men gave them pamphlets. Yates old desire for knowledge rekindled and he devoured the literature reading late into the night. He learned the Klan was:

A democratic and just organization which not only talks, but ACTS.

A secret organization. No one will know that you are a member.

To bring about total segregation of the races and the total destruction of communism.

To revive a Christian-like brotherhood among men in America.

One pamphlet said: *There comes a time in every man's life when he has to choose between the right or wrong side of life.*

Yates wanted to make the right choice. Only W A S

Ps could join – White, Anglo Saxon, Protestant men. They must be of high moral character and eighteen-years-old. Of the qualifications for membership, Yates lacked the last one. That would happen in a month on September seventeenth – the day he turned eighteen.

Yates decided that Pa was misguided thinking this group of men were bad. Just like he was wrong not to sue the doctors and get help for his leg. He was probably wrong about a lot of things. And if there really was a God, Yates would please Him when he helped the weak, innocent, orphans and widows. Though he didn't really care what Pa or God thought right now, Yates made up his own mind and chose to join.

He and Guy saved their money. Even though they could have paid the initiation fee in four installments they wanted to be men and have all the money at once. When they reached the proper age, they paid the ten-dollar fee, bought their robe and hood, and took the oath of secrecy. They were Klansmen with their names on the secret rolls.

Yates intended to participate in everything the Klan did to make people do right. Little did he know in the beginning all that it entailed. By the time everything was revealed to him, which came in small pieces, his mind was warped to accept all of the teachings, hook, line and sinker.

The two boys learned the secret handshake. If an unfamiliar person gave them the Klan handshake, they knew he was in the brotherhood.

A secret code they learned was AYAK, which meant, *are you a Klansman?* When they asked a stranger, if he answered *YIAK*, meaning, *yes, I am a Klansman*, they knew he was one of them.

Yates thrilled about all the good he would do. He longed to tell Roby and Gilbert, but couldn't. Roby didn't approve and Gilbert was drinking too much. Besides, if they knew, they might tell Ma and Pa before Yates had a chance to prove his point.

These Klansmen often took the law into their hands. That seemed innocent at first to Yates and he still believed he made the right choice. Even so, he sometimes got a funny feeling in the pit of his stomach when he was away from them and thought about it.

A gang of men were assigned to beat up a man who cheated on his wife. They had to teach him to obey the Bible. *Thou shalt not commit adultery.*

The first time Yates helped, he felt like a real man. He and Guy joined four others. They met after dark in the woods and put on their robes and hoods. Yates stashed a pint of whiskey in Guy's car and at the last minute, slipped a shot.

They waited across the street, hidden in a patch of woods, and watched for the offender's car. When the headlights appeared and his automobile rolled to a stop, they ran out and surrounded it. Enough light from the street lamp allowed them to see his face with his jaw dropped and his eyes wide and round.

One of the Klansmen snatched the door open and told him to get out of the vehicle. The man whimpered, "Don't hurt me."

"Yeah, like you didn't hurt your wife? Ever think how she feels with you out messing around with another woman?"

The leader pulled him out of the car and two of the

men dragged him across the road behind the bushes. The rest of the men jumped him, shoved his face up against a tree and tied him. Yates and Guy took turns with the others and flogged him with a leather belt. When his shirt was good and bloody the leader quietly said, "Don't ever run around on your wife again. Understand? We won't be so gentle next time."

Going home, Yates and Guy discussed the look on the man's face when he saw all the men in their white robes. Guy laughed and Yates joined in and said he didn't think they had to worry about him cheating again.

Yates was on his way to being a good American Klansman and figured someday Pa would see the light about the Klan and be proud of him for joining. He also realized that not one time that night had he thought about his limp.

The second time he took an assignment, things got out of hand. Word got around that this man was beating his wife and children.

The man was a giant sporting huge muscular arms. He towered above Yates who stood at six feet. This one didn't beg for mercy. When Yates slugged him, he stood square on the ground like a rock. Before Yates could move, the rascal hit him so hard in the nose that it jarred his teeth. When Yates regained his balance, he swung and punched while blood ran down his face. Several of the Klansmen joined him and together they beat the sinner to the ground.

Yates felt good about what he did even if he got a broken nose in the process. His nose eventually healed though it stayed a little crooked. He figured he lived with a short leg; he could handle a crooked nose, too.

* * *

Yates learned that the Klan actively opposed Negroes, Jews, Roman Catholics, and Orientals having the same privileges as white men. The Klan fought dope, bootlegging, rustling, violation of the Sabbath, prostitution, adultery, questionable business ethics, or any other scandalous behavior that did not adhere to the ideals of one hundred percent Americanism.

The Klan taught that all white men north of Mexico knew that black men were ignorant and second rate that they just as soon kill white men as to look at them and they would rape the white women. They said, "You white men can't let the niggers hurt your families. If they get away with that, they'll try to take your jobs. Next, they'll get into politics and take over the country. It'll ruin America."

The Klansmen taught them, "You better hate a white trash nigger lover as much as you hate the nigger. He gets a bad beating, too, because he's a traitor and has let America down. If he continues to associate with the nigger, then we burn a cross in his front yard. You know what that means." Yates knew it meant the man who associated with Negroes had better stop this time or he wouldn't live long enough to talk to another one.

Yates was learning things that Ma and Pa hadn't taught him at home. Things he needed to know to make his neighborhood and country better, more civilized. One of the pamphlets entitled, "Why You Should Become a Klansman," said they had to help keep America American.

Yates heart pounded the first time he helped burn a cross in the yard of a Negro who had been too friendly with a white woman. Word was out that he had raped her. A couple of men went first and planted the wooden cross in his front yard.

The others arrived chanting. Nobody could identify them hidden from head to toe in their white robes and hoods posing as ghosts of dead Confederate soldiers circling the cross. From every man's hand flamed a burning torch in the shape of a small cross. Together the Klansmen touched their lit torches to the bigger cross covered with burlap and doused with kerosene. It burst into white hot flames that leapt into the night sky and made a glow for miles around.

Chills went down Yates' spine, the fumes thick enough to taste. The men stood silent like statues with their robbed arms stretched, their awe-filled faces fixed on the cross. Yates felt proud to be a part of something this important. Something that made people do right. He wanted to tell, but knew that for the rest of his life, he had to keep it a secret.

He also knew that if he ever wanted to leave the Klan he was as good as dead.

Dollie

1920-1929

Eight

1920

The sun shone brightly on a lovely day in Tampa. Six-year-old Dollie hummed happily in her own back yard. She shoveled wet sand into her bright red bucket. When it reached the top, she dumped the dirt beside her other sand art, extending her creation. She patted and smoothed until the structure looked to suit her. Depositing a cup of wet sand onto the top, she made a dome, and then drew squares for windows and doors.

"Done!" She sat back on her haunches and cocked her head to the side. "That's beautiful." Leveling the ground around the base, she said to herself. "Someday I'll live in a big house just like that."

Suddenly a foot interrupted her peaceful reflection as it landed directly in the middle of her sand castle while the other foot rubbed half of it away. Butch, a neighbor boy grinned triumphantly down at her.

Dollie jumped up. Her eyes blazing, she brushed sand from her backside and ran at her tormentor screaming, "Look what you've done! You've ruined my beautiful castle."

Butch took off across the yard singing to the top of his lungs, "Nanny, Nanny, Bee Bee! Dollie can't catch me." He ran another lap around the yard and stomped the remainder of the sand palace into the ground. Dollie's dark brown eyes glowed with anger.

"I'll fix you, Mister." She snatched up an empty coke bottle and hurling it with all her might caught him squarely in the center of his forehead.

"Oh-h-!" He screamed, wiping a grubby hand across his face. "Blood!" It smeared on his fingers and trickled down his face. "I'm telling my Mama on you."

"You're a big ole' baby," she yelled. "Go tell your mama. See if I care."

Butch ran as fast as his feet would take him sobbing all the way, "Mama, Mama, Dollie's hurt me!"

Before long his mama, Irene, came scurrying down the street, apron strings flapping, the boy running along beside her a bandage on his head. "Janie Carter," Irene shouted, "come out here this minute!"

Dollie's slim mama appeared at the door dressed as always in the latest fashion.

"Look-a-here what Dollie has done to my boy's head. You need to whip that girl."

Janie came out of the house with her hands on her hips. "Now wait just a minute, Irene." She shook her head. Her curly, bobbed hair bounced. "I'll do no such thing. Your boy asked for it and I say it's good enough for him."

"What in the world did he do to deserve a bottle to the head?"

"I'm sorry, Irene, but he's mean to Dollie, everyday. I'm sick and tired of him coming in *our* yard aggravating the life out of her."

"Are you telling me he started this?"

"Yes, I am. And if he can't play any nicer, then you

need to keep him home." Janie looked at Butch. Blood seeped through the bandage. Her tone softened. "Oh, that does look bad." She took a closer look. "I'll have to admit my child does have a bad temper. Looks like it got away from her this time. I'll give her a talking to, but he still needs to leave her alone. I'm tired of hearin' about it day in and day out."

Irene pointed her finger, "Butch, go to the house, now! I'll tend to you later."

He ran sobbing and muttering, "I'll get Dollie good for this."

Irene turned and faced Dollie's mama. They were silent for a moment. Finally Janie said softly, "I just made a pitcher of lemonade."

The two women sat in wooden rockers on the long porch that spanned the front of the house and drank their cool, refreshing beverage. Rocking, they looked out over the velvety carpet of green grass and smelled the honeysuckle growing on the lattice at the end of the porch. Together they admired Janie's beautiful flower beds bordering the house. Soon the conversation turned and they discussed the pitfalls of raising children. With another dispute settled, they were still friends.

When darkness came and the trees looked like monster shadows in the yard, Dollie remembered the red blood running down Butch's face. In bed, she covered her head with her sheet and thought about it. She felt ashamed and afraid.

Dollie's hot temper was the reason Joseph Allen Carter, her father, playfully called her his Little Spitfire Doll.

Nine

1926

Allen Carter a short, small man had strong opinions and was not afraid to give them voice. It was believed his slightly red hair denoted a high strung temper, though he seldom let it get out of control. For the most part, he was kind and his demeanor commanded respect.

He never missed a day's work at the Cigar Box Factory. In spite of being a hard worker, his clothes were always clean and pressed. He was not afraid to help with the daily housework that many considered women's work. He set the table, washed dishes, washed clothes, swept the carpet under the dining table with a broom and once a month took it out to the clothes line to beat the dust out. He performed the manly chores too; trimmed the hedges that ran the entire length of the house, climbed a ladder to cut the dead branches from the palms that stood at the corners of the property and every Saturday mowed the lush St. Augustine grass with a push mower.

Allen and his family rode the street-car to work, the store and any place too far to walk, but suddenly, the motor car was all the rage. Henry Ford made it possible for the average family to own one. Production time for a car had decreased from twelve hours to one and a half hours and finally to twenty four minutes. This brought the cost down from eight hundred and fifty to three hundred dollars each. The company had even established a new way of paying called an 'on time plan' where people paid for the car in monthly installments.

One night at supper, Allen dipped a helping of collards and buttered a piece of cornbread. He turned to his wife, "Janie, we'll build a garage first before we buy a motor car. Can't have it sitting out in the sun and rain, you know."

"Do we have enough money saved for both?" Janie asked. She knew good and well that her husband would never buy anything on the new installment plan that people were jumping into. "If you don't have the money to pay for it when you buy it what makes you think you'll have the money later," he had said upon hearing about the new system called credit.

"We're getting a car?" Dollie jumped up from the table and gave her daddy a big hug. "Oh Daddy, are we really getting a motor car?"

Allen nodded and smiled. "Yes Dollie."

"Sit down, Dollie and eat your supper," Janie said. "No use getting so excited. It'll ruin your digestion. Besides, it won't be today. Like your Daddy said we have to build a garage first." Still Janie could hardly suppress her own excitement about the automobile.

"Can I drive it?" Dollie asked sitting down.

"When you're older, we'll see about it," Allen answered. "I don't know yet if I can drive a car. Never have tried." Turning to his wife he said, "Janie, if I can't learn, do you think you can drive one of them newfangled things?"

"I expect I can, Allen," she answered. "Not much to it, I hear."

"Bet I can," piped Buddy, Dollie's ten-year-old brother.

Dell, the older sister slung her hair back and batted her eyes. "I'll be the first to drive since I'm a teenager."

"Well, if you can drive, I can, too." Dollie replied. "I'm *nearly* in my teens, smarty."

"I doubt that, Scaredy Cat. You'd be too afraid." Buddy taunted. "She's scared of her own shadow," he said looking from one to the other around the table.

"I am not!" Dollie glared. "I'm not scared of you and I'm not afraid of driving a motor car." She turned up her nose at him.

Janie brought in a steaming peach cobbler diverting their attention for the time being. The subject rested as they dug into the mouthwatering dessert.

Soon a crew of men swarmed the back yard with saws, hammers and lumber. They measured and cut. The sound of hammers hitting nails and driving them into the wood rang out across the neighborhood. In a few days a wooden garage stood behind the house with the large opening of double doors facing the side street. A smaller door at the other end opened into the back yard. Another group of men arrived. They poured cement to make a walkway from the garage to the back door of the house. Everything was ready and waiting for the new motor car.

The Saturday they went to purchase the motor car dawned clear and bright. Dollie nearly exploded with excitement. She dressed carefully and was the first one ready to go. "Hurry up, slowpoke," she taunted Buddy.

He gave her a cuff on the arm. He and Dollie ran to join the rest of the family. They all strolled to the next corner and boarded the street-car that took them to the Ford dealership.

Allen and Janie carefully considered their choices and selected a Model T. Allen held his head high when he paid cash. None of that credit business for him.

The salesman gave Allen a crash course in starting a Tin Lizzie and warned him to take it easy as the car could go at the unsafe speed of 40 to 45 miles an hour.

"Never mind about that," Allen said, "I intend to go slow."

Step by step the salesman walked him through the difficult process of cranking the car.

"Be careful when you turn the crank," he warned. "If it kicks back you can sprain your wrist or break an arm. You need to cup it in your hand like this." He demonstrated with his hand in an upward position. "This way will sling your arm away from the crank if it kicks back. Were you to grab it with your thumb on top, the rapid reverse motion will violently twist your wrist."

Allen nodded his eyes bright. He reached in the car and set the spark and throttle just as the man instructed him. Next he went to the front, stuck his finger in the loop of wire that controlled the choke, pulled the loop and simultaneously turned the crank with all his might. It took several times until at last the engine roared. Then he leaped to the trembling running board, leaned in, and as the salesman directed, moved the spark and throttle to the proper position. Wet with perspiration and a little shaky, at last he was at the wheel with both wrists intact.

He chugged out of the car lot and into the road. Unsure of himself, he swerved back and forth across the dusty road hitting potholes instead of missing them. Bumping along, the car shook, rattled and rolled. Janie wanted to cry out several times but, ladylike, she kept her peace. Dollie, Dell and Buddy in the back seat had a hard time trying to smother their giggles as they bounced along. Now and then Dollie chirped, "Watch out, Daddy."

Janie put her finger to her lips and said, "Shhh."

Finally, they arrived at the street leading to their house. Allen swung out too far to make the turn, went into a shallow ditch, up the other side and hit a tree.

"Now look what I've gone and done!" He got out to inspect for damages. Janie stayed in the car head still erect trying to suppress her laughter.

Dollie climbed over Buddy's legs from her spot in the middle of the back seat and opened the door to get out. Janie quickly made her get back and stay put.

Dell snatched her skirt from under Dollie and smoothed it. "Sit still, Dollie, and stay off my dress. You'll have it dirty and wrinkled."

Dollie gave her a look and stuck her nose up in the air. "Make me," she said.

Allen climbed back into the car. "Well, I've gone and made a dent in the front fender before I got the bloody thing home."

Dollie put her hand over her mouth to keep from saying anything.

Janie looked out the window, her lips curled in a smile.

Allen backed the car off of the tree, put it in the

road and headed for the house. When he arrived, he stopped at the garage entrance and crawled out. "Janie, you'll have to park this ornery thing and from now on, *you'll* do the driving!" He slammed the door and stomped toward the house.

Janie calmly slipped over to the driver's side and eased the Model T. into the garage. From that moment, she was in charge of the driving. She took Allen wherever he had to go. He cranked it for her, but that day was the first and last time that Allen Carter ever drove a motor car.

Though he never drove again, Allen didn't lose his dignity. It never appeared the least bit, to bother him. He accepted it as a fact of life; he didn't drive and that was that. His family respected him the same and his authority as head of the house did not diminish one iota.

Ten

1927

Janie Carter was a pretty woman and a little taller than her husband Allen. She kept her hair bobbed and curled in the latest style. Her clothes were good quality and fashionable. She had an even temperament and was sure of herself. Not harsh or bossy, she kept everything under control, the house, the children, the job and the motorcar.

An industrious couple, Janie and Allen rose every morning at 4:30. While he kindled a fire in the wood cook stove, she put on the coffee pot and started mixing and patting out biscuits. The children awoke to the delicious aroma of coffee perking, bacon frying and biscuits baking. Allen set the table then sat in his chair and read the morning paper, The Tampa Tribune, while Janie finished cooking grits and eggs. Homemade jelly was always on the table in a variety of flavors: strawberry, blueberry, guava, or grape for the fluffy hot biscuits with real homemade butter.

When everyone finished eating, they all helped wash dishes, make beds, and sweep the floors. The house was spic and span before Janie drove herself and Allen to work at the factories. They arrived by 7:00 A.M.

After work she swung by the farmers market and

bought fresh collards or turnips, fruit and vegetables. Arriving at 13th Street, she stopped at the Banana Docks to meet the boats from South America. She would not be without bananas. Once home she cooked a big supper and made more homemade biscuits. Again everyone pitched in to clean the kitchen.

On warm days, which were almost every day in Tampa, after they finished their work, Allen and Janie sat on the front porch in their big rockers to cool off in the evening breeze. The children took the swing at the end of the porch. Allen spat his tobacco juice far out over the porch into the grass. Janie tried to be discreet with her snuff. In a small brown bag, she placed an empty can and hid it under her chair. When she thought no one was looking she eased it out and let the brown juice run out of her mouth into the can.

The children told about their day at school and Allen and Janie discussed politics and other subjects they heard at work from the readers – men hired to stand or sit on a platform at one end of the huge factory room and read to the workers. In the mornings they read about politics and current events. In the afternoons they read classic novels and other entertaining stories.

At dusk when the mosquitoes began to bite, the family stopped their talking and rocking and went inside.

On cool winter evenings, the family stayed in the house, built a fire in the fireplace and listened to the radio or played records on the Victrola until bedtime. At 8:30 Allen banked the fire, Janie locked the doors and everyone went to bed. After a good night's rest, the next day started like the last. They lived a quiet, peaceful life of hard work and held high moral standards, but church was not included in their Sundays.

One day when Janie and Dollie had finished their weekly shopping in Ybor city, a Cuban section of Tampa, Dollie peered into a store window.

"Mama, look at those red shoes! Aren't they the cutest things you've ever seen?" Dollie bounced up and down. "I just gotta have 'em."

"Dollie, those are high heels."

"I know and they just match my new red dress. Please, Mama!"

"Dollie, you're only thirteen. That's too young for high heels."

"But, I'm a teenager. Besides, they're the latest style. I could wear them dancing."

"Dancing! You're too young to go dancing."

"I dance at the house all the time. After school, before you get home from work, Dell and I wind up the Victrola and dance all over the living room." Dollie twirled around on the sidewalk. "I'm good at it, too, Mama. You should see me. Please, can I buy the shoes?"

"No, you can't and that's that." Janie ended the conversation and walked toward the car.

Dollie stomped along behind her. "Oh, Mama," she wailed.

Janie turned the handle at the front of the Model T and cranked the engine. She climbed in and Dollie followed slamming her door. They pulled out of the parking space and bumped along on the burnt-red brick road heading for home in silence. The only sound was the chugging of the engine. Janie's mouth was drawn in a tight line; Dollie's eyes wet with tears. As soon as the car rattled into the garage and stopped, Dollie jumped out and ran for the house. She passed the blue hydrangea bush at the back door and entered the enclosed porch letting the door slam behind her.

"Daddy, Daddy!" She ran through the house and found him on the front porch. He had completed his usual Saturday morning chores of mowing the yard, sweeping the dining room rug with a broom and whatever else Janie needed him to do. He rested in his cane bottom rocker, a plug of tobacco in his hand. Knife open, he cut a chunk, dropped it into his mouth and began to chew.

"Daddy, we're home." She hugged him and smelled the familiar scent of tobacco and a working man's sweat. That was her Daddy and she loved him.

"Hey, Doll," he said. "You and your mama have a good shopping trip?"

"Oh, Daddy," enthusiasm bubbled in her voice. "I found the *cutest* pair of shoes. They're the *latest* fashion."

"Well, show 'em to me." He chomped on the tobacco.

"Mama wouldn't buy them for me." She stuck out her lower lip in a pout and rolled her dark brown eyes. "I want them, Daddy. Can I have them? Please."

Allen scratched his head and looked thoughtful. He wondered why Janie hadn't bought the shoes. She had the money. They both worked hard to provide for their family; she hand-rolled cigars at Hav-a-Tampa and he made the small sturdy boxes that housed them. They were not rich, but they earned a steady salary, certainly enough to buy Dollie the shoes.

Janie came through the house and onto the porch. She gave a long sigh and fell into a matching rocker, her purse strap still across her forearm. Opening the purse, she found her snuff can and removed the lid. She turned away from Dollie, tilted her head back, pulled out her bottom lip and dumped in a small amount of the powder. Placing the lid on the can, she slipped it in her purse and asked Dollie to stash it away in her closet.

With Dollie out of earshot Allen spit a wad of ugly, brown tobacco juice across the porch and out into the well-manicured lawn. It barely missed the row of yellow marigolds that lined the porch and landed in the thick St. Augustine grass. "Janie," he cleared his throat, "why didn't you buy Dollie the shoes she wanted?"

"Allen, they were high heels. She's too young for that."

"She's a teenager now. You've got to let her grow up."

"I know. But she's so tiny. I'm afraid she'll get hurt in them." Janie shifted in her chair.

"You've got to let her live, Janie. Can't baby her all of her life. I think you ought to take her back to the store and get her those red shoes."

Janie thoughtfully reached under her rocking chair and pulled out her small brown bag with an empty tin can. Turning her head away from her husband, she let the brown liquid drool out her lips and into the can. She wiped her mouth with the back of her hand, placed the can in the bag and out of sight under the rocker.

"All right, Allen," she whispered and sighed.

Dollie jumped up and down when she heard that she

could have the red shoes. Back to the store they went. The shoes were a perfect fit and Dollie admired them while Janie paid the bill. Dollie wrapped them in their paper nest and placed them in the box just right so they would not get scratched.

At home again she ran past the blue hydrangea bush, through the house and out onto the front porch. "Here they are!" She smiled and pulled the shoes out of the box. Holding them up she ran her fingers across the ankle strap. "Daddy, look at the straps that go across the ankle with the tiny button on the side. I just love that and the fancy stitching on the heel." Sticking her feet into the shoes, she buttoned the little clear buttons and spun around and around while Allen Carter admired them.

She danced over to his rocking chair, set on the arm and raised one foot with her leg straight out. "Oh, Daddy, aren't they pretty? I'm going to wear them to dances." To test the shoes again, she did the Shimmy across the porch.

Allen Carter cleared his throat and spit tobacco juice flinging it way out in the yard. Finally he leaned back in his rocker and smiled. "They're bloody good red shoes, Dollie. I like um."

Dollie flung her arms around his neck. "Oh, thank you, Daddy!"

Eleven

1928

Dollie longed to meet her Grandmother Carter who lived in Spain. All of her life she dreamed of the day when the elegant lady her daddy told her about would appear on their doorstep and walk into her life. She daydreamed of Grandmother's compliments about how sweet and pretty Dollie had grown. She imagined, and could almost hear her speak the encouraging words that grandmothers were supposed to say.

At last the day came when Grandmother Carter sailed to America, and moved in with Dollie's family. Dollie was thrilled to see that she bore a strong resemblance to her Grandmother.

When Allen introduced his family, Grandmother Carter gazed at Dollie's sister Dell.

"Look how beautiful you are," she said. "Turn around and let me see you. Si, si, you're as gorgeous as your cousins in Spain." Then she went into a long discourse describing their beauty and accomplishments.

She finally turned to Dollie and said, "Now let's look at you." She looked over her glasses at Dollie. "You're a skinny little thing. It's too bad you didn't get your sister's good looks."

Dollie was crushed.

One evening at the supper table, Janie passed the fried chicken, mashed potatoes, and fresh green beans and was about to start the biscuits.

"I just don't understand it." Grandmother Carter started in again on the subject while dipping a spoonful of the fluffy mashed potatoes.

"What's that, Mother?" Allen Carter took a biscuit from the plate and passed it.

"The difference between your daughters." She pushed her mashed potatoes into a neat pile then made an indention for gravy. "We come from a long line of beautiful Spanish women. One of your cousins who came to this country was so pretty she became a star in silent movies. Dell is pretty like her." She looked at Dollie who listened intently. "I simply can't imagine why Dollie is not pretty, too."

"Mother! How can you say that?" Allen said sternly.

"Because it's true."

Allen banged a fist on the table. "Mother! That's enough. It is not true."

Dollie jumped up from her chair and ran from the room. She flung herself onto the bed sobbing into her pillow, "I hate you!"

She was tired of hearing her grandmother say that she was not pretty. Sick of being compared to Dell – *Dollie is not as good at the piano as Dell – Dollie is not as smart as Dell – Dollie is not as pretty as Dell.*

She wondered what was wrong that her own grandmother didn't like her.

* * *

After Grandmother Carter came, she insisted that the females of the family observe tea at three o'clock each Saturday. One of those afternoons when Janie and the girls finished weeding Janie's colorful flower beds of gladiolus, marigolds, zinnias, pansies and chrysanthemums that surrounded the house, Grandmother made her weekly announcement, "Let's all go out on the *piazza* for tea."

"All right," Janie said. She stuck the last scarlet poinsettia, cut from a bush in the back yard, into her arrangement and placed it on the dining table. Cocking her head to the side she admired how beautiful it appeared against the white lace cloth.

Dollie sighed as she filed out of the house with her sister. She and Dell took the swing and glided back and forth. Everything was peaceful as they gazed at the white planters atop low red brick walls flanking the front steps. In the pots, blue hydrangeas made a splash of color against their vivid green leaves.

The girls' attention was drawn away as Janie held the door open for Grandmother Carter who emerged carrying a tray laden with cups, sugar, lemon slices and a teapot. She poured and served the steaming drink. She and Janie settled in the green rocking chairs to gaze at the plush yard that lay before them like a flat emerald carpet. It was a picture postcard on the corner in a quiet and well-kept neighborhood; just the place to enjoy a cup of tea on a peaceful Saturday afternoon.

At first, the two women exchanged small talk as they sipped their beverage. Then Grandmother's sharp eyes began to observe and again compare the two girls. Before long, she sighed and said, "It's just too bad that Dolly's not pretty like Dell."

Hot tears of anger sprang to Dollie's eyes. She jumped out of the swing, swallowed hard and faced her grandmother. "Everybody says I look just like you!"

Grandmother gasped. "No, you don't!"

Dollie's eyes flashed. "Go to hell!"

"Well, I never!" Grandmother Carter arose blinking rapidly. "How dare you talk to me like that!" She stormed into the house, the screen door banged behind her.

"Joseph Allen," she said through clenched teeth, "You have to do something about Dollie. Do you know what she just said to me?"

Allen, sitting in the living room, had overheard it. "Yes I do," he said. Out onto the porch he went with Grandmother at his heels.

"Dollie, I don't like what you said to my mother. You will respect your elders. I want you to apologize to her."

"But Daddy," Dollie sobbed, "she said I'm not pretty like Sister. She says it all the time. She makes me feel ugly."

"What you said was wrong. Apologize."

Dollie raised her head, tears streamed down her face. "Sorry," she said halfheartedly.

"Now, Mother," Allen turned and faced her, his eyes blazing. "Don't ever again say that Dollie is not pretty! She is beautiful."

"Why, Allen Carter! Don't you use that tone with me!" With her hands on her hips she shook her head. "I'm your mother!"

"And I'm Dollie's father!. I've stood by and listened to you pick on her from the moment you arrived and I'm sick and tired of it. Don't ever say it again!"

Grandmother Carter raised her head with a jerk, "Hump! Don't expect me to stay where I am treated like this. I'll not stand here and take it." She stomped into the house and slammed the bedroom door.

Soon Grandmother Carter packed her trunks and left to live with other relatives. Dollie breathed a sigh of relief as she walked through the quiet house where peace reigned once more.

From then on Dollie hated the woman she was named after as much as she hated her name – Dalsedia. She was glad everybody called her Dollie, even if her daddy did add "Spitfire."

* * *

"Hey, Bird Legs!" Butch yelled as he ran to catch up with Dollie and her two girlfriends. They walked home from school and each one carried a load of books.

Dollie turned and stomped her foot, cocked her head to the side and wagged her finger at him. "I told you that's not my name."

"Yeah, yeah, but you're no bigger than a bird." He came up behind her and tugged her bobbed hair. "How much do you weigh, Toothpick."

She glared at him and put her hands on her hips. "I'll have you know I weigh 86 pounds, so there." She made a face and resumed walking.

He quickened his pace and walked beside her. "Big deal. You must've gained a whole pound since you started high school." He grabbed her books and grinned. "Here,

give me your books. You're not big enough to carry them."
After a few silent steps he said, "Bet you can't guess what I saw yesterday."

"What?"

"Your picture in the drug store window."

"You're lying!"

"Am not. It was right there pretty as you please, advertising Ivory soap - 'For velvety beauty of skin,' like yours."

"I don't believe you." Dollie shook her head.

"Oh yeah? Come on and I'll show ya." They walked a few blocks to the drug store. Her photograph stared from the window big as life, proclaiming that by taking a face-bath with Ivory and warm water, followed by rinsing and a dash of cool water, every woman could have a beautiful complexion that radiates the natural glow of cleanliness. With Ivory, the velvety beauty of her skin would be remembered.

The bottom of the picture declared in gold letters, Dee's Photography.

So, Uncle Frank Dee is responsible for this.

How she wished Grandmother Carter could see her picture advertising Ivory Soap. That would show her. But then Grandmother's words rang in her ears again and Dollie knew she would never be pretty enough or good enough to measure up to her sister, Dell.

Twelve

After her sister Dell married and moved away, Dollie was afraid to sleep by herself. In the quiet, dark room, old fears haunted her. Sleep came easier when the nightly routines of her parents, soothed and comforted and made her feel secure, but date nights were different. The heavy silence when she entered the house at her ten o'clock curfew, her father's soft snore and the solitary bedroom made her feel as if something was about to happen again.

She wasn't exactly sure what caused her apprehensions. Maybe they began when she was a little girl and neighborhood bullies, older and bigger, taunted and teased. Sometimes they hid behind a bush and leaped out roaring with laughter as her eyes widened with terror. She jumped, screamed and ran, her terrified cries echoing down the deserted street. Or they would catch her from behind, poke her in the ribs and mock her when she threw a fit, balled up her fist and swung at them. All of this made her a quivering bundle of angry nerves.

Maybe her awful terror began one dreadful night in her childhood when the house two doors down from where she lived caught fire. She could still see the flashing lights and hear the scream of sirens that awakened her in the middle of the night. At the sound of all that commotion she leaped out of bed and ran to find her parents but couldn't. Their room was empty.

She raced outside to an uproar of people, trucks and lights. Neighbors poured out of their homes and stood watching as a house went up in flames. Dogs, roused from sleep, barked and howled.

Dollie thought she'd grabbed her daddy's leg but when she looked up the leg belonged to a stranger. She turned it loose and ran, crying loudly for her mama and daddy, but all she saw were firemen dressed in bulky rubber suits and helmets. They shouted to one another and rushed about hooking up a huge hose to the water hydrant on the corner where her house stood. They sprayed the burning home, but the house continued to blaze.

Smoke filled the whole area. Dollie coughed and choked until she could hardly breathe. Covering her nose with the sleeve of her nightgown, she watched the red and yellow flames leap high into the midnight sky. They roared out of control engulfing the whole house until it fell apart before her eyes.

The worst part of all, the thing that caused her panic for years to come was the helpless feeling she had when she couldn't find the family who lived there. The little girl, Ann, was her friend.

For days, she breathed the sickening stench of burning flesh; an odor unlike anything she had ever smelled. Weeks afterwards, the odor still stung her nose. It seemed her body had absorbed it and the smell followed her everywhere she went. There was no getting away from it.

Sometimes she wondered if the shriek she heard

that night was from the fire truck that came too late to rescue them or if the sound was the yell of the family and her friend Ann trapped in the blazing house.

Often she relived the scene in a nightmare and awoke with the stink in her nose, the scream in her head, her body wet with sweat and her pillow soaked with tears.

Adding more fear Dollie heard stories about the house her parents lived in before she was born. It also burned down. Allen and Janie built it back in the exact spot on the same corner. *What if it burned down again and she was in it? What happens to you when you die? Where was her friend now?* These thoughts, intensified by the darkness, tormented her.

On nights Dollie didn't date, the normal routines soothed her. Insecurities faded when she and her twelve-year-old brother Buddy turned off the crystal radio and shut the lid on the Victrola. Her daddy always took the clock from the mantel, wound it and set it back in its place. In the wintertime, he banked the fire in the fireplace while her mama latched the screens, then shut and locked the wooden doors. The routine was comforting and sleep came easily on those evenings.

The nights she dated, when she came home and let herself into a dark house, she felt unsettled. She closed the door, put on her nightgown, and crawled into bed pulling the covers over her head.

One night after finally drifting off to sleep, she heard the crackling of fire and the mournful moan of a siren. Was she dreaming again or was the house burning? Terrified, she jumped out of bed and ran to her younger brother's room. When she sat on the edge of the bed, he turned over and bolted upright.

"Get out of my room!" He hit his fist against the mattress.

"Buddy, I'm scared!" Dollie whispered. "Just let me stay till daylight."

"No! Ain't no girl gonna sleep in my room."

"Please. I dreamed about the fire again."

"I don't care. Go on back to your room, scaredy cat."

Dollie turned to go wishing with all her might that Dell were still home. Why in the world did she marry Paul and go off to live with him?

"If you're old enough to date, you're old enough to sleep by yourself." Buddy called after her.

Dollie tiptoed back to her room and sat on the edge of the bed. She wrapped the covers tightly around her body and, with eyes wide, tried to see in the dark. After what seemed like forever, she crept back to Buddy's bedroom door and listened for his breathing. When it was regular and she knew he was sound asleep, she tiptoed into his room. Holding her breath, she eased onto the edge of the bed and lay as still as a brick. Not moving a muscle all night, she barely slept. When the first rays of sun appeared, she headed back to her own bed, her fear swept away by light of day.

She sighed in relief. *Another night and he didn't know I was there.*

Thirteen

1929

Five evenings in a row and most of Saturday, Janie Carter sat at her Singer sewing machine. Her legs pumped the treadle up and down until her muscles groaned, stiff and sore. She created long rows of one-inch wide ruffles for a special pale yellow dress. Sixteen ruffles covered the bell shaped skirt from the waist to the hem, just below the knee. Lace covered a sleeveless, scoop-neck bodice that was topped by a lace stole.

To complete the outfit, Janie and Dollie found white shoes tipped with pretty yellow ribbons that matched the dress and tied the straps together in a bow at the top of each foot.

Students of Jackson Heights High School nominated Dollie to run as Queen for a Day. The contest was a big annual event. If she won, Dollie would represent her school and ride on a float in the Gasparilla Parade.

Mama Carter wanted her to be a source of pride for the school as well as the family and was willing to sacrifice the time to see that she had a proper dress. She looked lovely in that dress and Allen felt confident that his Spitfire Doll would win, but Dollie was not so sure. She wondered how she could ever win anything after Grandmother Carter told her so many times that she just wasn't pretty.

Dollie held her breath as the school officials counted the vote. The whole school was in an uproar. The contestants sat on the edge of their seats, waiting to hear the announcement. One at a time, the students yelled the name of their favorite participant. A boy in the crowd started a chant, "Bird Legs, Bird Legs, Bird Legs." Soon the crowd took it up. Dollie felt her face flush, and knew it must be red. How dare Butch humiliate her like this. And he was taking her to the Gasparilla parade.

"We'll just see about that!" she muttered.

The school principal called the assembly to order and asked Dollie to come to the front of the auditorium. Was she in trouble because of the ruckus? Everyone knew that, Bird Legs was what a few of the ornery boys called her. She held her head down all the way up the long isle.

To her amazement, the principal placed a dainty white flower circlet on her head. Tiny white ribbons, interwoven with the flowers, met at the back of her head and hung in a long tassel. Her cheeks flushed and she caught her breath when he crowned her announcing, "Dollie Carter, I pronounce you Queen for a Day!"

When she stepped off the platform, Butch rushed to her side. "Congratulations Dollie!" He picked her up and swung her around. "Don't forget, I'm your escort to the parade."

"Don't be so sure of that." Dollie put her hands on her hips. "You made everybody call me Bird Legs!"

"Aw, Dollie, that's because you look so cute when you're mad," he said and winked. "We all like you even if you do have skinny legs." He lifted her chin and looked into her eyes. "You're the bees' knees, Dollie."

He looked very handsome at that moment, and he was a great dancer. "Okay," she smiled, "I'll let you escort me." She touched the scar on his forehead. "Guess I owe it to ya for that."

The day of the parade dawned without a cloud in the sky. To introduce the festivities, well-to-do business men, playing the part of pirates, sailed up the bay while hundreds of smaller boats, crammed with spectators, followed them up the waterway.

The scar-faced, swashbuckling imitation Pirates wearing eye patches were named Ye Mystic Krewe of Gasparilla. They were rich businessmen. With open liquor bottles in hand, and firing blanks from huge, booming cannons and smaller guns, they stormed the city. Finally, amidst great whoops of triumph from the cheering crowd, the mock war ended and Tampa's mayor presented the key of the city to the pirate captain. Since 1904, the pirates had won this imaginary battle with the City of Tampa.

The parade began on Bayshore Boulevard, one of the city's major streets, and ended in downtown Tampa. Shooting blank pistols, the Krewe threw beads, coins and trinkets from the floats to the cheering crowds that lined the streets several humans deep. Parked Model T's and Model A's formed a continuous row down street after street.

Gasparilla Festival was a safety valve for the immigrants. It was a risk-free way for them to express their resentment. The War of Independence in Cuba, which lasted for ten years, was responsible for 100,000 Cubans fleeing their homes. Many of the poorer people were workers in the cigar factories. They first came to Key West, Florida, which was only ninety miles from Cuba by ship.

Trade-union militancy resulted in one of the Cigar factories at Key West being burned. The owner was a Spanish businessman from Havana named Vincent Martinez Ybor. After the fire, he moved the factory location from Key West to Tampa transferring 2,000 workers with him, and established Ybor City, making nearly half of Tampa's population. A good natured, paternalistic boss, he reigned over his workers of Cubans, Spaniards, and Italians. Under his direction, the workers helped finance the Cuban revolution by giving one day's wage of their weekly salary.

When Ybor died, the American Cigar Company bought his factories. The good- natured, personalized capitalism ended, replaced by an industrial era dominated by the drive for efficiency.

The birth of the Gasparilla Festival came at this time of ethnic and social tension. Immigrant Cigar workers could relate their own situation to the pirates who came in and took what they wanted, then shared their wealth as they gave the treasures back. The city's businessmen allowed it on this one day of the year as long as the pirates were Tampa's businessmen.

Dollie rode on the school float that she helped cover with white crepe paper. Posed on a white wrought iron chair, she looked like a fresh yellow flower. Smiling, she moved her small hand gently back and forth as she waved to the crowd of excited people. She turned to greet the onlookers from each side of the street, her eyes bright, wishing with all her might that Grandmother Carter could see her now.

Many of the participants were Spaniards. A lady in the crowd yelled something in Spanish to Dollie and she turned her head away. *What makes that woman think that I can speak her language?* Old resentment and anger toward Grandmother Carter, her name and her nationality surfaced. *I should have been born French!*

Flanked by the tremendous crowd, the Spanish lady was soon out of sight and Dollie forgot her anger. She felt exhilarated by the partying parade that ended in a street festival. Many vendors sold drinks, food and all types of pirate goodies. Drinking, dancing, and partying in the streets created an energy level that was electric.

At the end of the Parade, after three hours of sitting on the float, turning, waving and smiling to the sound of beating drums and horns from the bands, Butch met a happy but dazed Dollie.

"Let's get something to drink," he said taking her arm and steering her toward one of the booths.

"I'm kinda hungry. Could I have a Cuban sandwich and a Coke?"

They found a place to sit on a nearby low wall. The food revived Dollie and she talked excitedly as they waited for nightfall. The day had been like a fairy tale. She found it hard to believe that all this was not just a dream.

When it grew dark, the glow and sparkle from fireworks lit up the beautiful Tampa Bay skyline. Dollie looked at Butch and his handsome face shone in the glow. She glanced down at her lovely yellow dress, illuminated by the flashing fireworks. Dollie held her head higher. She looked like a queen, and for a moment, she even felt like one.

A reporter approached and asked to take a picture of the good-looking couple. They posed, smiled and the camera clicked just as thousands of sparkles cascaded over their heads. Dollie couldn't wait to see the print in the local paper. She would be sure to send a copy to Grandmother Carter.

Kidd
and
Dollie

Together

1930-1933

Fourteen

1930

Yates entered the drugstore pausing near the doorway. A girl, with other teens, stood at the soda fountain counter sipping a Coke. She turned and looked at Yates. Her flashing black eyes captured his total attention. He stared unable to move or breathe. A tiny thing, she stood about five feet two inches tall, a head shorter than his six-foot frame, perhaps weighing all of eighty-five pounds. Yates estimated her to be about sixteen years old, two years younger than he.

She turned back to talk to her friends. Yates finally drew a breath and watched her for a few seconds more. Today was the first time he ever saw her and he liked her. He liked the fire in her dark eyes and he liked her dark brown hair. He liked her quick answers and energy. She appeared daring and exciting, yet she acted innocent and child-like. Right off Yates wanted to protect her as he would a tiny kitten.

His friend Bill Townsend stood next to him.

"See that girl in the red polka dot dress?" Yates said in a low voice, "I'm going to marry her."

"Who, Dollie?"

"Her name is Dollie?"

"Yeah, that's Dollie Carter."

"Dollie." He rolled the name on his tongue and liked the feel and the sound. "Fits her to a T," he mumbled. "She *is* a doll."

Yates tucked his white shirt tighter into his pants and touched the wave in the top of his brown hair making sure it was still in place. Hoping she wouldn't notice his limp, he ambled over to her as evenly as possible. "Hey, Doll." His voice was soft, smooth, "How 'bout goin' out with me tonight?"

"Who are you?" she looked right at his crooked nose, broken in a fight.

Yates held his breath. He'd hoped she wouldn't notice, but his confidence soon returned.

"Oh, excuse me," he bowed and spoke in his most gentle tone. "My name is Yates – Yates Warren Kidd."

"Yates?" She tossed her head. "Where in the world did you get a name like that?"

"Named after Dr. Yates; Ma's doctor when I was born." He squared his shoulders and stood a little taller.

"Oh." She raised her eyes and looked straight into his, making his heart flip. "Well, Yates, I can't go out with you tonight. I already have a date with Butch." She pointed to a boy standing a few feet away with a slight scar on his forehead, a fellow Yates knew as E. T. Fox.

"Are you talking about Ed?" Yates asked.

"You know him?"

"Yeah. You need to go out with me, not him."

"Sorry, we already planned to go dancing at the club.'"

Dollie read the disappointment on his face. "Come

over to the club and I may give you *one* dance." She emphasized one by holding up her index finger. Then, playfully, she flipped his chin with that tiny finger.

Yates heart sank. Dance? He couldn't dance. Not smoothly, anyways. Still, he wasn't a quitter.

"I'll be there," he said, flashing a big smile that revealed the wide gap between his two front teeth. *And I will dance.* Yes, he would be at that dance and all of the Friday night dances if that's what it took. While lying in a hospital bed all those months he had developed a good deal of patience. He could wait.

"See ya, tonight, Doll." Yates turned and walked away struggling to make his gait smooth.

"Yeah, if you're lucky," Dollie called after him.

The minute he walked into the club Yates saw Dollie. She was doing the Charleston, smiling and moving to the music as if she were born to dance. Ed wasn't doing too badly, either. They made a striking couple. A jealous tingle ran through Yates until Dollie looked up and smiled. Still he couldn't tell if she actually smiled at him or just for the joy of dancing. Either way he noticed for the first time that she had a part in her two front teeth just like his. *It's a sign. We are meant for each other.*

Soon as the music stopped, he was at her side. "This is the dance you promised me," he said as the orchestra played a slow song. He could make it on that kind of music but not the fast, jazzy stuff. He took Dollie by the hand, put his other hand on her tiny waist and led her onto the dance floor keeping his weight on the ball of his right foot trying not to limp. "You know something Dollie?"

"What?" she said looking into his eyes innocently.

"I'm going to marry you."

"Are you crazy?"

"No." He pulled her close and whispered. "I'm going to marry you. You'll see."

She shook her head, pulled back and laughed. "You *are* crazy. I'm not old enough to get married."

"How old are you?"

"Sixteen. How old are you?"

"Nearly nineteen." They turned and swayed to the music. With his head bent towards hers, he caught the scent of Dollie's perfume. It sent his senses reeling. "Sixteen is young but I'll wait. I've got the patience of Job."

"Who in the world is Job?" She looked up at Yates, puzzled.

"A man in the Bible."

"Oh, really? I've never read the Bible."

"You didn't go to Sunday School?" Yates questioned.

"No," she said blushing. "My folks are Catholic but we never go. Do you?"

"I used to. Not anymore."

"I went to church one time with a friend." Her eyes got bigger and her voice more animated. "Got so scared, I promised myself that I would never go again, if I got out of there alive." She drew a little closer to Yates. "They really acted crazy. People called 'em Holy Rollers."

"I know all about them," he nodded.

"You seem to know a lot of things, Yates." She tilted her head playfully. "Like who you're going to marry."

"Will you marry me, Dollie?" He gazed into her eyes his heart in his throat.

"I might." She winked. "Depends on how long you can wait."

"I'll wait forever for you, Doll."

She laid her head on his chest for the rest of the dance. Yates wondered if she heard his heart pounding. His chin rested on the top of her head as they swayed to the music.

She 'might' marry me? I know she will.

Fifteen

Yates stopped the car in front of Dollie's house. While walking up the sidewalk, he admired the well kept yard and flowers. It reminded him of his Ma, who loved flowers, too. He arrived at the door and knocked. A small, neatly dressed man appeared behind the screen. "What can I do for you?" he asked.

"I came to see Dollie." Yates' voice slightly trembled.

"Can I tell her who's come calling?"

"Yes sir. My name's Yates Kidd."

The man opened the screen and shook Yates hand. "Nice meeting you, Yates. I'm Allen Carter, Dollie's father."

"Nice meeting you too." Yates nodded and hesitated to say more.

After a long awkward silence Allen said, "Would you care to come in for a visit?"

Yates stepped inside their tidy living room. Two overstuffed chairs and a sofa took up most of the room. A fireplace stood on his right flanked on each side by bookcases with glass doors. Sunlight streamed in through two small windows, one above each bookcase. On a table by the front window sat a lamp, a figurine of a woman in a

147

long skirt and, folded neatly, the morning newspaper – *The Tampa Tribune.*

Beyond a wide opening, a large dining room held a formal table covered by a lace tablecloth. A centerpiece of fresh cut flowers put off a faint floral aroma. Both rooms were in perfect order and immaculate.

"You can sit there, young man." Mr. Carter motioned toward one of the big upholstered chairs.

Yates sat on the edge of the seat. "Nice place you have here." His voice cracked.

"Thank you." Allen Carter sat in the other chair. "We worked hard for it. That's the only way to have anything."

"Where are you employed, sir?"

"Cigar Box Factory," he replied. "Been at it since I was a boy. Have to work and save up for a rainy day, you know. Don't want to end up in the poorhouse."

"That's right, sir. I work hard, too. Have since I was twelve. Plan to buy a nice home like this myself someday." Yates looked around the rooms again.

"That sounds good. Keep laboring and you will. Don't ever depend on other folks for what you need. Work for it." He balled up his fist and beat the air for emphasis.

"I intend to, sir."

"What did you say your name is?"

"Yates Kidd."

"Well, now, Yates, you came to see Doll, did you?" He chuckled. "It's too bad she's not here."

Yates lifted his brows his eyes grew wide. "She's not here?"

"No, but since you seem like a nice young man,

maybe I'll just tell you where she is."

* * *

Dollie and her friends splashed and played in the lake most of the Sunday afternoon. The sun was way past the middle of the sky and long shadows from the huge oaks that lined the sapphire water told Dollie it was getting late. She decided on one more swim before she drove them home, pulled herself up onto the dock and ran out to the end of the diving board. Raising her hands above her head, she sprang up on the end of the board and with a nimble leap, bent her body and sliced into the water as gracefully as a dolphin.

Around her the water was clear and sparkled where the afternoon sun filtered through the trees and landed in patches on the surface. She swam out several yards before turning around, and then flipped over to do the backstroke. Closing her eyes, she relaxed and floated in the pleasant warmth of the afternoon. Too soon, the sun's rays touching the end of her nose began to cool. Time to leave, she decided. She floated toward the shore wiping lake water off her lids with the back of a hand and opened her eyes.

Yates stood on the end of the dock grinning at her. Dollie was shocked to find him in a swim suit, his shoes off, his shirt opened as the tail of it waved in the breeze. Balancing his body weight on the ball of his right foot, he called out, "Hey Doll, you're quite a swimmer."

"What are you doing here?" Dollie said treading water.

"Looking for you. I came to go swimming with you." He yanked off his shirt and slung it to the side. "Then I'm gonna take you home with me."

"You're not taking me anywhere." Dollie's eyes

flashed fire.

A pretentious look of fear swept across Yates face. "Look out, Dollie! Behind you."

Dollie screamed and thrashed around expecting to see an alligator, but the water was calm, nothing in sight. She heard Yates laughing and her friends joined in with him.

Her friend Mabel called out, "Get him for that, Dollie. I'll help you."

"I don't need your help!" Dollie yelled.

She charged out of the water and in one fluid motion, pulled her body up onto the dock. Yates watched her, fascinated by her energy. She stopped at the end of the dock, sizing him up and catching her breath. All at once, he grinned at her, spreading his hands out as if he expected her to tumble into his arms.

Like a charging bull, she ran at him, positioned her shoulder right in the middle of his stomach and pushed with all her might. He plopped into the water with a big splash. Dollie lost her balance in the struggle, toppled into the water and nearly landed on top of him. They both came up sputtering. When Dollie could see again, she swam away as fast as she could a long ways out in the lake. She turned around, treaded water and saw that he followed her.

"You nearly drowned me," he said.

"I will drown you if you scare me again."

In a tender voice he said softly, "You don't have to be afraid of a gator or anything else with me around, Dollie. I'll take care of you." He took her face in his hands and kissed her gently on the lips. Water lapped around their chins and up on their faces. She kissed him back and tasted the faint flavor of alcohol.

"I'm crazy about you, Little Doll," he whispered.

She pulled back and looked into his steel gray eyes. They were not a cold gray for they twinkled, alive with mischief. "You can't be crazy about me, you don't even know me." She looked down at the water.

Suddenly a big smile crossed her mouth and she hit the water with her hands forcing it into his face and up his nose.

"Race you back to the shore," she called as she swam away with long even strokes.

He snorted and slung his head side to side like a wet dog. Launching forward, he easily caught up with her and swam stroke for stroke by her side. When they neared the shore, he sped up and stood on the bank when she walked out of the water.

"No fair," she said. "Your legs are longer than mine."

Mabel and Dollie's other friends were waving, yelling and cheering them on.

"He beat you fair and square, Dollie." Mabel said. "We were watching."

"You don't know anything, Mabel." Dollie took a towel and dried herself. "It's getting late girls. We'd better head for home."

The girls gathered their things and walked toward the car leaving Yates and Dollie alone. Dollie offered Yates her towel since he didn't have one. He wiped his face, shoulders, and arms and reached for his shirt. She grabbed the towel from him and dried his back. "You can't put your shirt on a wet back," she mumbled.

He liked her rubbing his back and wanted to turn around and take her in his arms but it wasn't the time or place. He picked up his shoes and escorted her to the Model T walking on the ball of his right foot.

"Go out with me tonight, Dollie," he said on the way to the car. His eyes twinkled. "We need to get to know each other better since we're going to get married."

"I never said I was going to marry you."

"You like me though, don't you? Come on admit it."

"Well . . ." she rolled her eyes, "Maybe a little. But that doesn't mean I'm going out with you."

"Come on, Dollie," he pleaded, "Pick you up at seven? We'll go dancing."

Their eyes met and he gently touched her cheek.

"All right," she said barely above a whisper.

"Atta girl." He opened the car door and she got in. He poked his head in the window. "I'll get the crank for you." As he walked to the front of the car, he added in a playful tone, "You're too little to turn it yourself."

She stuck her head out of the window. "Who do you think cranked it for me to get here? I'm not helpless you know."

He laughed and nodded. "Yeah, I know."

When he heard the chug of the motor, Yates walked back to the car window. "But you still need me." Their eyes met again and this time Dollie smiled.

Yates face grew solemn, "Be careful driving this automobile, Dollie. These vehicles can be dangerous. I don't want you to wreck and get crippled up like me."

"Oh, don't say that. You're not crippled. You can

walk."

"Yeah, with a limp." He looked down.

"Listen to me, that limp is barely noticeable. Besides, you can dance. That's all that matters to me. See you at seven, Yates." She waved, put the Model T in gear and rattled down the road, her girlfriends hanging out the window, calling out their goodbyes.

"He's cute," Mabel said. "If you don't want him, I'll take him off your hands."

"You leave him alone, Mabel." Dollie's eyes flashed.   "He's   mine."

Sixteen

Yates knew that Dollie expected him to keep his word and take her dancing. He didn't enjoy it the way she did. It was hard for him and made him feel uncomfortable. She was good at it. He wasn't. The only part he enjoyed was holding her in his arms. He would go through anything for that privilege.

When he got to her house she came to the door in a red dress designed in the latest fashion with a long waist and a sash around her slender hips. The sash was tied in a saucy bow on the side and the skirt flounced out from the hip line. She wore matching red shoes with high heels.

Her hair, combed close to her head, was parted in the middle with finger waves down each side and a roll of hair across the bottom of her head. Red lipstick was all the make-up she wore. Her flawless complexion required nothing else.

To Yates she looked like a real live doll. His mouth went dry and his heart skipped a couple of beats. She glided out the door and Yates took her arm to escort her to his vehicle.

"You look beautiful," he whispered in her ear.

She glanced at him, smiled shyly and lowered her eyes.

Yates wanted her to himself for a while before they

went to the club, away from all the noise and other men who would cut in to dance with her. When they got in the truck, he suggested the two get a bite to eat at a quiet place.

Dollie frowned. "You said we were going dancing."

"We are."

"Then why do we have to stop and eat. I ate supper at home."

"I didn't and I'm hungry."

She wasn't buying it.

"Look, Dollie, I know a little place you're going to love."

"What's the name of it?"

"The Goody Goody on Florida Avenue."

"Oh, I've heard of that and been wanting to try their butterscotch pie." Her voice filled with excitement. "They're famous for it."

"Good." Yates put the truck in gear and headed in the direction of the drive in restaurant. Dollie insisted they go inside instead of eating in the truck. They took a table for two beside a window. Looking out at the building next door, Yates saw a huge sign sprawled across the brick. There in bold letters, beside the menu for the Goody Goody Drive In, he read a warm message for newcomers to the city.

Welcome to Tampa, Florida.
Our people come from all over the world.
Pioneers long ago with vision and sacrifice ordained the building of this city.
Here you will find rest, strength, new hope and courage.
Tampa is the gateway to the west coast of Florida.

Yates felt a lump in his throat. "Look at the sign." He pointed.

"Yeah, it's just the menu," she said and turned around.

"No, the part beside that - the Welcome."

She looked again and this time read it aloud. "That's nice," she said when she finished.

"The third line tells why my family came here." As he remembered his eyes felt misty. "At least, the reason my Pa came," he added.

Dollie read the line again. She questioned Yates with her eyes.

"He was real sick. But he found help here in Florida. He's well." He didn't really want to talk about Pa, not tonight, so he turned the conversation to her. "Has your family been here long?"

Dollie smiled and nodded. "We've lived here all of my life. I like it, but would love to see other places, too."

"Someday," he put his hand over hers, "I'll take you where ever you want to go."

The waitress interrupted with Yates' jumbo hamburger and onion rings and Dollie's dessert. As they ate, he could tell from the little 'umm' sounds that she liked the butterscotch pie so he made a mental note to take her there again.

When they arrived at the dance club Dollie was moving to the music before they were out of the truck. She headed straight to the dance floor with a friend they met on the way in and while she was occupied, Yates went to the bar for a shot of whisky.

After a while the music changed and Yates took Dollie in his arms. The couple floated across the dance floor to the sound of the orchestra's howling horns and wailing strings accompanied by the slow steady beat of the drums. Yates barely noticed his limp and felt that he could accomplish anything with the girl he held so close to his heart.

Dollie broke the spell. "How did you hurt your leg, Yates?" she asked

Yates told her about the accident and the months he lay in a hospital bed, flat on his back and all wrapped up like a mummy.

"That must have been real hard for a strong man like you." She said her eyes warm and tender.

Encouraged to talk by her rapt attention he explained further, "One of the doctors experimented and failed. The other one was drunk when he operated on my hip."

"Oh, my goodness!" Her eyes grew bigger. "Can't something be done about it?"

"Pa was advised to sue both doctors for making such blunders. With the money he could have hired better doctors to fix it, but he didn't."

"You must be real mad at him for that."

Yates swallowed hard, nodded and tried to sound like it didn't matter. "It's nobody's fault, really."

Then he pulled her close and whispered in her ear, "I love you, little Doll." They slowly swirled and dipped to the music. Yates knew more than ever that he wanted this girl for his wife

Seventeen

Yates thought of Dollie constantly. The more he thought the more he determined to win her over. He boasted again to his friend Bill that she would soon be his wife. The process began by taking her often to the one place that delighted her most – the dance halls.

When the band played the Charleston or the Black Bottom, Yates sat at a table and watched Dollie do her favorite thing. It gave him an opportunity to drink. Sipping from the short, fat glass of bourbon made him feel mellow and took the edge off his longing to be out there with Dollie. He didn't mind as much that his legs wouldn't maneuver to the jazzy music.

Dollie could literally dance all night. One night she nearly did. That Friday night when she came back to the table after dancing the Shimmy, Yates asked her if she was ready to eat, but her blood was on fire from the music. She shook her head and sang along with the band.

"Where the blue of the night meets the gold of the day, someone waits for me." She warbled the words like a little canary and tugged at his hand. "This is a slow one, dance with me, Yates."

How could he resist? He abandoned his drink, took her in his arms and pulled her close. She snuggled against his chest singing softly while he whistled a gentle accompaniment, both lost in their own little world of dreams, unaware of anyone else in the room.

When the dance ended the romantic mood lingered as they joined their friends, Bill and Mabel. Dollie surprisingly accepted the drink Bill offered. After the first one she drank and danced for hours, she and Yates lost in each other were unaware of the time.

Dollie, who wasn't used to drinking, suddenly grew dizzy. The room spun and her face turned a peculiar shade of green. She ran to the ladies room. After a long time she returned to the table pale and listless.

"I need to lie down, Yates. Would you take me home?" Then she asked about the time.

Yates looked worried. "It's two in the morning."

She moaned, "I can't go home this time of night."

"I'll go with you to face your parents."

"No! Mama and Daddy can't see me like this. I'm drunk!" She hiccupped. "What am I gonna do, Yates? I can't go home! I just can't. . . Ohhh! Why did I drink so much?"

"It'll be all right, Dollie."

"No it won't. Don't you understand? I can't disappoint them." She put both fist to her eyes and rubbed them looking exactly like a child.

Yates laid his hands on her shoulders and looked her straight in the eyes. "I have an idea," he said softly.

"What?"

"Let's get married tonight, then you wouldn't have to go home."

Dollie pulled away and shook her head, "Don't be

silly. I haven't finished school yet." She swayed, Yates grabbed to steady her.

Mabel staggered over to them and butted in, "Heck, it don't matter if you've finished school or not." She hiccupped.

"It does, too." Dollie's words slurred.

Bill stepped up. "The old folks couldn't do anything to you," he pointed his finger, "if you went home married."

"No, I can't. Didn't you hear? I'm too young!" Dollie's voice grew louder. People around them turned and stared.

Yates lowered his voice for her ears only. "I'm crazy in love with you, Dollie."

She opened her eyes wide. "Love?" She swayed and he caught her again. "I do love you, Yates, but I'm still too young to get married."

"Heck, you're seventeen." It was Mabel again.

"That's too young, Mabel and you need to mind your own business!"

Mabel totally ignored the remark. "You dumb cluck, you just said you love him. Why don't you marry him?" Mabel shouted.

"Shut up, Mabel. You don't know nothing. You can't get married at seventeen. Get that through your thick head."

"Then tell 'em you're eighteen. Shoot, we'll lie for you and sign the paper." Mabel pointed her finger in Dollie's face. "I dare ya to tie the knot with Yates tonight."

Bill butted in again. "I double dog dare you!"

"How about a triple dog dare?" Mabel added and weaved. Bill steadied her.

Yates took Dollie by the hand and led her away. "I always take a dare, Dollie. Will you marry me now?"

Dollie looked at Yates for what seemed like eternity then she giggled, grabbed him around the neck and yelled, "I'm gonna marry Yates, tonight."

People at the tables nearby who had heard the conversation began to clap and cheer. Dollie took a bow and waved yelling, "I'm gonna marry Yates." He took her hand and escorted her from the dance hall. Bill and Mabel followed them out waving to the crowd.

They left for Sulphur Springs where Bill knew the Justice of the Peace. The four banged on the door, laughing and carrying on until he came. Still pulling on his robe and rubbing his eyes with hair all tousled, he ushered them into his office where he consented to perform the ceremony. In his home, at three o'clock in the morning, and half drunk, they said, "I do." Not really the way Yates had planned this big event, but it didn't matter to him, as long as he had Dollie.

* * *

The couple found a room to spend what remained of their wedding night. Yates closed and locked the door, stripped to his underwear and crawled into bed holding the covers back for Dollie. She stood by the bed fully clothed staring at him.

"What's wrong, Dollie?"

Her eyes glistened in the dim light. "I'm scared."

"Of what? Your parents?"

"No," she whimpered, her chin quivering.

"What then?"

"I don't want to tell you." Her eyes filled with tears

and began rolling down her cheek.

"Dollie, you can tell me."

"I can?"

"Sure, I'm your husband now. You can tell me anything."

"Really?"

Yates nodded. "What is it?"

He barely heard her murmur, "I've . . . never . . ." She looked away. "It might hurt."

"Is that all you're worried about?"

She nodded.

"Come on to bed, Dollie. I'm not going to hurt you."

She sat on the side of the bed for a while then pulled her feet up and lay down, clothes and all. Drawing the sheet to her neck, she lay straight and tense.

The disappointment Yates felt made his heart sink. He had won her hand in marriage but decided this was another area he had to win. He would *not* force Dollie. When she came to him it would be willingly not because he was the stronger of the two. He had already learned that sometimes in life we must wait. He decided that this part of Dollie was worth waiting for until she was ready.

Yates reached over and kissed her gently on the cheek. "I love you, Dollie. Good night." With that said he turned his back to her and went to sleep. There would be plenty of time for lovemaking after she was used to the idea of being a bride.

Eighteen

The next morning the couple arose and dressed. Yates wanted to go by the fish market before he faced Dollie's father. When they arrived, her parents met them at the door. Worry lined their faces and Janie's eyes looked a little swollen. As soon as she saw them, Dollie blurted out, "We got married last night!"

"What?" They answered in unison, with gaping mouths and their eyes stretched wide.

Janie's voice finally returned. "We were worried to death about you, Dollie."

"I'm sorry, Mama," Dollie hung her head.

Yates handed her father the package he had gotten from the market. "I didn't come empty handed, Sir. Here's Dollie's dowry."

Allen took the package and eyed it suspiciously. "What's this, Yates?"

"Something you like."

He pulled the newspaper back to reveal a big trout. He burst into laughter and the last trace of worry faded from his face. "Is this what you think my daughter is worth? One fish?"

"No, sir," Yates grinned. "There's a lot more where

that one came from." Yates grabbed his new father-in-law's hand and shook it hard.

Allen pulled Yates into his embrace. "Welcome to the family, Kidd. I know you'll treat Dollie right, provide her a good place to live." He paused then continued in a softer tone. "Glad to have you for a son-in-law."

"Thank you, sir." Suddenly, feeling shy, Yates hung his head.

"Well, I'm relieved that you two are all right." Janie gave them both a big hug. "Come on in, Yates. I'll cook you and Dollie some breakfast." She took the fish and headed for the kitchen. When it was safely in the icebox to keep until supper, she put on a pot of coffee and took out the frying pan. Soon the aroma of bacon and coffee filled the cozy kitchen. Creamy white grits boiled in the pot while bacon and eggs sizzled in the skillet. She popped a batch of biscuits into the oven and set out homemade butter and jam.

Dollie poured a cup of steaming coffee for Yates. He put his arm around her waist and mentally counted his blessings: She was his bride, her parents knew they were married, and they accepted him into the family. This hearty breakfast with them was the perfect start for a good marriage.

Yates thought, *the only problem is where in tarnation will we live?*

Nineteen

Toward the end of the delicious breakfast, Janie poured the newlyweds a second cup of coffee, "You two need to go down to Frank Dee's studio today and get your picture made." She put the coffeepot on the stove. "Someday your children will want to see your wedding picture."

"Wedding picture?" Dollie batted her eyes. "But we didn't have a wedding." Her chin quivered. "We went to the Justice of the Peace in the middle of the night." She burst into tears. "I'm married and I didn't even have a wedding!"

Yates hurried to her side and put his arm around her shoulder. "It's all right, Dollie," he consoled. "Who needs a big shindig? We're just as married without one."

"But . . ." she looked up at him and said through her tears, "I always dreamed of wearing a beautiful white dress and veil with a big party afterwards . . . and dancing." She laid her head on the table sobbing softly.

Janie flushed wondering if she had spoken out of turn with her suggestion of pictures. Apologizing, she tried to reassure Dollie's new husband. "She's just tired from all the excitement and lack of sleep, Yates. She'll be all right in a bit."

Minutes later, Dollie composed herself, dried her

tears and washed her face. Her beautiful skin needed no powder but she dabbed the puff on her nose anyway and touched her lips with red lipstick. Just a hint of rouge on her cheeks and her grooming was complete. She pulled on her best red dress and patted her shiny dark brown hair in place. Looking in the mirror she turned each way to make sure she looked right for her photograph with her husband. *After all, this is my wedding day.*

Yates splashed his face with water and followed it with shaving lotion,. He donned his three-piece suit, dragged the comb through his hair and patted the wave on top. Off the couple dashed to 7th Avenue in Ybor City and Dee's studio, with both still a little hung over from the night before.

Weeks later, when he viewed the photographs, Yates grinned. The few times he witnessed Dollie drinking booze he noticed the next day her left eye squinted, making it appear smaller. Sure enough in their wedding picture Dollie's left eye was smaller than the right one creating a permanent memory of their drunken spree the night they married.

Twenty

The day they made their pictures Yates decided he had put something off too long. After leaving the studio he took Dollie to meet his family and tell them they were married. Pa and Ma grabbed Dollie in a big hug and welcomed her to the family. His brothers and sisters gathered around.

Yates' brother Sam looked her over. "How'd you ever get her with your ugly mug, Yates?" he joked. "You sure picked a pretty girl."

Dollie blushed, then said, "Yates' mug is not so ugly. He looks like you." They all laughed. Dollie hugged each one, feeling accepted by every family member, as Yates introduced her to his seven brothers and sisters.

Ma made plans right away for Sam and James, the two brothers born after the family moved to Florida, to give up their bedroom for the newlyweds, but Yates had different ideas. He knew they couldn't squeeze in there to live. There was no privacy and very little room. He wanted something better for his Doll, a quiet retreat like the house where she grew up. They would find a place of their own.

After discussing it, Dollie explained that her Mama and Daddy would let them stay in her room until they found a house.

Back at the Carter's Janie and Allen eagerly gave

them permission to stay while they looked for a place.

"This is only temporary," Yates said as he hauled his clothes through the door. "We won't stay with you long."

"Stay as long as you need to," Allen said.

Janie nodded. "We have room, Yates."

The next day found the couple house hunting. Yates felt they couldn't afford much. Though he already worked hard, he decided to get a second job. He meant to give Dollie the best.

They found a little two-bedroom bungalow in Jackson Heights, two blocks from Dollie's parents. They rented it but the excitement dwindled when Dollie saw the dirt and grime inside. She wasn't about to move in until the house was spic and span.

In her usual demonstrative way she expressed her dislike. "Yates, I'm not going to live in filth," she said. "You'll have to help me get this place cleaned up."

"I will, Dollie. Before you know it we'll have our first bungalow in tip top shape."

The next day was Saturday. Starting at sun-up they wiped down the walls, then headed to the store for paint. Yates asked Dollie to select the color. "You know more about that kind of thing than I do."

She remembered an art class at school and selected an off white that looked close to pale yellow. "This is neutral which means it will go with any other color," she said happily. "Plus it looks sunny and cheerful." Looking at him hopefully, she asked, "Do you like it Yates?"

"Suits me fine." He nodded his head and reached in his pocket for the money. "Let's get it."

They worked all day and most of the next. By the middle of the week, the walls looked fresh and clean, a shiny new linoleum rug lay on the living room floor and new soft curtains hung gracefully at the windows.

Janie and Allen came to inspect the young couple's first house and declared it ready for occupancy. They gave Dollie her old bed and a table with chairs from the sun porch. Dollie's brother Buddy helped move them. Little by little, as they could afford it, they would add other needed furniture.

Dollie looked around when everything was settled and the two were alone. Pale yellow walls sparkled clean, muted yellow roses on tan linoleum in the living room gleamed, and yellow and white curtains fluttered in a gentle breeze blowing softly through the windows. A pot of blue hydrangeas sat on the table with a crocheted scarf beneath it.

Dollie grabbed her new husband's hand. "Doesn't this place look better than when we first saw it, Yates?"

He smiled and agreed.

Dollie let go of his hand twirled around and did a few dance steps then took a deep breath. "It even smells fresh." She grabbed his hand again. "Now I'm ready to move in."

Yates brought her hand to his lips and kissed it gently. "Me, too," he said. "Let's go get our clothes."

Dollie smiled. "Thanks for being patient with me, Yates. You're a good husband."

Yates' heart did a flip flop. He took Dollie in his arms and kissed her tenderly on her forehead moving to her temples then each rosy cheek. His lips made their way to her neck and finally her lips. She kissed him back again and again until they were both breathless. Finally he took her by the hand and led her to the freshly made bed in their little love nest. Once there she yielded to his gentle manner and the two became one flesh.

Twenty-one

One morning seven months after they said, "I do," Dollie announced at the table, "Something has made me sick, Yates. Every morning after you leave for work I throw up."

Yates, busy eating his breakfast, just grinned. "Really?"

Dollie toyed with her grits and eggs. "Why are you grinning at me like that? Is something funny? I feel awful and all you can do is sit there with a silly smile on your face?"

"Pass the butter, please," was his only reply and, still beaming, he dropped a pat of butter into the hot biscuit.

"Something terrible is wrong with me." Dollie worried. "I just don't feel right."

Yates couldn't wipe the grin off his face if his life depended on it. "You'll be all right in about nine months."

Dollie frowned at her evasive husband. "Nine months! What are you talking about?"

"A baby, Dollie, you're going to have a baby. Can't you see that?" Elated he grabbed her hand from across the table. Angrily she jerked it away.

"How do you know so much?"

"Cause my Mama did the same thing. She had eight, you know, five after I was born."

"My mama didn't throw up before Buddy was born." She continued in a loud voice. "Nobody even knew she was that way until the last couple of months."

"Well, my Mama got sick every morning, even if yours didn't." Yates calmly continued to eat his breakfast, taking big bites of his biscuit while Dollie fumed.

"I don't want to have a baby right now." Her chin quivered. "I'm too young. Besides, I want to go dancing. How can I dance . . . with a big belly?" She said between whimpers. "I'd have to stay home. I don't want to stay home. I want to go dancing." Dollie put her head in her hands and cried.

"Think about it, Dollie," Yates laid his hand on her back, "a baby, a son." But her breath came in long hard sobs. "I'll help you take care of it. I helped Ma with her babies." He rubbed her back soothingly. "Anyway, you can still go dancing a while longer."

She calmed her crying a bit. "I can?"

"Sure. You can still dance for a while."

Finally, Dollie lifted her head and wiped her eyes on her apron. "You really think so?"

"I know so. I'll tell you what: let's tell your Mama and Daddy. We'll go right after work."

"Think they'll be excited?"

Yates nodded and said, "Yeah."

When he arrived home, Dollie had supper waiting as usual. They ate quickly, cleared the table, washed and dried the dishes. No matter how bad she felt, Dollie would not leave the kitchen less than spotless.

They arrived at the Carter's house with Dollie looking a little weepy, but Yates still had the morning's grin on his face.

Dollie's eyes filled with tears again when Janie opened the door. "We've got something to tell you, Mama."

Janie took one look at Dollie. "You're going to have a baby."

Dollie blubbered. "How did you know?"

"Why, it's written all over your face." She hugged Dollie. "Don't cry. It's good news."

"No, it's not. I won't be able to go dancing."

"You're going to be a mother. That's more important than dancing. Besides, you won't be this way forever."

"Seems like forever to me. Oh, Mama, what's wrong with me? I love dancing better than anything."

"You'll be okay, I promise." Janie hugged Dollie again then added. "You and Yates can still go out on Friday nights. I'll tend to the baby."

"What's this I hear about a baby?" Allen came into the living room from the kitchen, drying his hands on a dishtowel.

Dollie turned to face him. "I'm having a baby, Daddy."

"Aw, that's great, Doll. Bet it'll be a spitfire just like you. Can't wait to get a-hold-of the little devil."

A tiny smile crept over Dollie's face. "You think I'm big enough to handle it, Daddy?"

"Course you are." He put his arm around her shoulder. "My little Doll can handle anything. Let's go sit awhile." He opened the front screen door.

While Janie went to her closet for a discreet pinch

of snuff, Dollie and Yates filed out into the fresh, sweet evening, Allen behind them. He settled in his favorite rocker and pulled out his pouch of chewing tobacco, cut off a piece and popped it into his mouth.

"Think it'll be a boy, Yates?"

Yates sat in the rocker next to him. "Hope so."

"Well, I wouldn't mind it being a little girl. Got a grandson already, you know." He looked at Yates. "Yep, a little girl would be bloody good."

Yates turned away and lit a cigarette. "You want a smoke to help settle your nerves, Dollie?"

She sat in the swing and shook her head. "You know I don't like the taste of them nasty things, especially now when I feel so queasy."

They stayed on the porch until after dark and talked about raising babies. Janie and Allen Carter spit their tobacco juice, Yates smoked his Chesterfields and Dollie toyed with the idea of motherhood.

Secretly, Yates thought about the added responsibility of the new little life he had fathered. He reminded himself how important it was for their child's protection that he stayed active with the Klan. Occupied with his new bride, he had neglected to attend all the meetings. That was about to change.

Twenty-two

Mama Carter expressed to Yates privately her fear that Dollie wasn't big enough to have a baby since she only weighed 89 pounds. Yates hadn't thought about it. His Ma had eight children and came through fine each time. But, he sure didn't want anything to happen to his Doll.

After morning sickness subsided, Dollie ate everything in sight and put on weight. Her once flat belly began to extend.

"Yates, look at how fat I'm getting." She rubbed her stomach.

"Yeah, you're a regular roly poly." He rolled his eyes and laughed. "Are you up to a hundred pounds yet?"

"Oh, Yates, I'm fat as a cow!"

"No, you're not. You're beautiful."

"But, I don't want to have a big belly."

"Don't worry. It'll go away after the baby's born."

"I'm sick of hearing, 'after the baby's born'." She mimicked. "You can go dancing . . . 'After the baby's born.' Your stomach will be little again . . . 'After the baby's born.' I want to be little now," she whined.

Dollie's words echoed in Yates' ears. He wondered if her complaints came from something other than the size of her stomach and her urge to go dancing. The problem could be fear - old fears added to new ones - like fear of childbirth, motherhood, the unknown, and his love diminished with her figure changed.

"I love you the way you are, Dollie." He took her in his arms and gave her a long and tender kiss shutting off any more complaints.

When he turned her loose she smiled and said, "As long as you still love me no matter what, I'll be okay."

After that, Dollie resigned to the fact that she was going to have a big stomach for a while, but it would go away and she could go out and dance again – after the baby was born. As days passed Dollie seemed to accept the fact that life changes with time and adulthood.

Finally the day came when little Dollie looked like all stomach. When the time of delivery approached, she was ready. No longer worried about her figure or going dancing, she just wanted it to be over. At last, her labor pains began. For several hours, she groaned and paced the floor, and then she asked Yates to take her to her mama's and get the doctor.

"Are you sure?" He knew that sometimes babies took longer to arrive than the mother expected.

"Yes, I'm sure!" She gave him a hard look. "Let's go!"

Yates had learned by now that when Dollie's eyes flashed fire, he had better get a move on. He helped her into the truck and took her to Mama Carter's house. She took care of Dollie while Yates rushed out for the doctor.

Dr. Dyer came with his black bag and ordered Dollie to bed. Mama Carter went to the kitchen to boil a pot of water. Yates went to her side as labor pains picked up.

"Ohhhhhh". . . . Dollie strained with all of her might. "I can't stand it."

"It's all right, Dollie." Yates took her hand to comfort her

"No, it's not," she said gritting her teeth. "It's killing me." She squeezed his hand until sweat popped out on his forehead. He squirmed. Her grip was like a vise.

"Nobody told me it would hurt this bad." She glared at her mama." Why didn't you warn me, Mama?"

"Now, Dollie it will be over soon," Mama Carter consoled.

"Try to relax," Yates tone was soft.

Before his eyes Dollie turned into another woman. "Try to relax!" She roared. "You!" she said through her teeth. Her eyes narrowed. "You did this to me." She gasped for breath. "Don't you ever touch me again! Do you hear me?" She made another low guttural moan, "Ohhhhh . . . I can't bear it."

Drawing in a breath, she filled her lungs with fresh air and pushed until her whole body shook. Yates blinked. Within seconds, to his amazement, a tiny bald head appeared.

"There it is, Dollie," the doctor said. "Give us another good push." Encouraged she gathered her strength to push again.

"Press against her knee, Yates. That will help her."

Using his free hand Yates pushed against the knee propped up on the side where he stood. The doctor reached for the baby's shoulders and finished delivering their first child. Dollie took a deep breath and let out a long low sigh letting the wind blow against her teeth. Her body went limp as she relaxed. A smile spread across Dollie's mouth, a smile so big that it transformed her face into a picture of pure joy.

The next thing Yates knew he heard a husky cry and the doctor said, "It's a girl!"

"A girl?" Yates frowned. He caught himself before disappointment registered on his face in front of Dollie. He would adjust. There was plenty of time to have a boy.

Dollie, relieved that the pain was over, watched fascinated as Doctor Dyer checked to see that the newborn had all of her parts. She lay quietly while Mama Carter washed the baby. Within minutes Dollie felt tranquil and contented with the baby at her breast. She smiled sweetly at Yates, love shining in her eyes.

"Isn't she beautiful, Yates?"

He nodded his eyes moist. "So are you, Doll." He leaned and kissed her on the forehead. Then kissed his new girl, the sweet baby that was an expression of his and Dollie's love; love that signified Dollie's desire for him as her husband. Suddenly Yates realized that he had enough love for both of the girls in his life.

He got up feeling exhausted, but at the same time so relieved. The worry had ended; Dollie was big enough after all to deliver their seven pound girl. They named her Norma Jean.

Though she wasn't the boy Yates had dreamed of, she was a tiny fragile thing who needed him. She was Daddy's little girl and he would become her hero. He promised himself right then and there, if she were ever sick or injured he would be sure to find the best doctors possible for his precious baby daughter.

Twenty-three

Life changed drastically with a baby in the house. After a while the couple got used to being a three-some, the crying, being up all hours of the night and the endless mound of dirty diapers. Dollie adjusted to motherhood and looked contented as she nursed, rocked, sang and talked baby talk to little Norma.

As soon as she grew old enough to leave with her mama and daddy, Dollie was ready to go dancing. Excitement filled her as she dressed and left with Yates for the dance hall. She whirled and twirled and felt like she was back in her element. Yates watched her on the fast songs, danced with her on the slow ones. His hip ached in between dances so he sat and drank.

A routine established and the couple dropped Norma off with Dollie's mama and daddy more and more until most weekends found Yates and Dollie at the dance halls.

Norma continued to grow. She learned to walk and talk. By the time she was two the dances became so frequent that Norma grew tired of being left and began to put up a fuss immediately when she heard them talk and make plans to drop her off again. The whining continued until they were dressed and out the door.

Soon Yates borrowed a policy from the Klan; a way to keep her from knowing they were going until the last minute. They abbreviated their talk. "NJMA" meant Norma Jean is going to Mama's. When Dollie wanted to go to a dance she used the code, Yates nodded and that night found them in the club. After using the method a few times, Norma's above normal intelligence decoded their secret message.

One day Dollie looked at Yates and asked, "NJMA tonight?"

To their amazement Norma blinked her big blue eyes and said, "No! I don't want to go to Mama Carter's."

They were stunned for a few moments, then they broke out in laughter. Dollie gathered Norma in her arms and promised her pancakes the next morning if she went to Mama Carter's without a fuss. At this age pancakes were her favorite breakfast food. After that she went willingly.

Several days in a row Dollie made pancakes for Norma and finally was tired of it.

"I want pancake." Norma whined the next morning.

"No, I can't make you one today." Dollie lied, "I don't have any flour."

That evening they dropped Norma off at Mama and Daddy Carter's house while they attended another dance. After Yates and Dollie left, Norma said, "Mama Carter, will you give my mama jes a wittle bit of fower."

"Sure, honey." She patted Norma on the head. "Your mama doesn't have any flour?"

"No, Ma'am." Norma shook her head and opened her blue eyes wide. "Her didn't have any fower to make me a pancake wif."

"I can give her some." Mama Carter smiled.

Norma was sleeping soundly when Yates and Dollie returned from the dance. Yates went in, gathered her up in his arms, brought her out and settled her on Dollies lap. Mama Carter followed him with a sack in hand.

"Dollie, are you all doing all right financially?" She stepped up to the window and handed her the sack.

"Sure, Mama. What's this?"

"Flour."

"What's it for?"

"Norma said you didn't have any this morning to make her a pancake."

Dollie's face turned red. "Oh, Mama, we have flour. I lied to Norma because I was tired of making them."

Mama Carter laughed. "You little rascal." Her face grew serious. "I don't want you to do without, Dollie," she whispered. "Let me know if you need something – anything."

"I will, Mama. Thanks."

But Yates knew she wouldn't. Her parents had taught Dollie to take pride in providing for her own needs and not to accept charity. Yates, too, was confident that they would make it on their own.

* * *

Dollie's figure returned to normal, her stomach flat again. But a few extra pounds from the pregnancy remained making her curves more appealing than ever. One day she purchased a new red dress for the dance that night. Before Yates came home from work she dressed and twirled in front of the mirror. Soft folds of fabric crossed on the front of the dress and draped at the neck revealing her shapely figure. Yates appeared at the door. His tall figure reflected in the mirror as he leaned against the door frame and admired the view. Dollie's pulse quickened and she fluttered over and kissed him.

He washed and dressed. After walking her to the truck he helped her in and told her how beautiful she looked. When he got in and cranked the motor he turned to appreciate the beauty of his wife once more. His smile turned to a frown. For some reason, he hadn't noticed the plunging neckline. There under his nose and in his face a large portion of her bosom was exposed. He knew how that would appeal to the men at the dance.

"You need to pin the neck of that dress, Dollie." He didn't want every man at the club leering at his wife.

She looked down. "It's all right, Yates."

"No it's not." He pointed his finger. "It's too low."

"It's fine!" Irritation sounded in her voice.

"It shows everything you've got."

"That's the way it's supposed to be." She tossed her head. "It's the latest style."

"I don't care about style." His jaw tightened. "Fix it!"

"No! Let's go, Yates." She crossed her arms.

He turned off the engine. "I'm not moving an inch until you pin up that dress."

Dollie flounced out of the truck and slammed the door. She was back in a few minutes still fuming, but with her neckline higher.

"Now my dress is ruined, Yates. I hate you for that!" She pouted, looking like a child.

I won that round. Yates grinned, knowing that when Dollie heard the music her feet had to move and her anger dissipate. He also knew that when he had a drink, he wouldn't worry about any of it.

Twenty-four

Yates sat at a table in the nightclub clutching a glass he kept hidden behind a napkin. He had promised Dollie to quit drinking, but he watched Dollie's eyes sparkle as she laughed and danced with Butch, and he raised the glass of whiskey and took another swig.

This is their third dance tonight.

Resentment started in the bottom of Yates gut and rose to his throat. He would never be able to twist and twirl and glide to keep up with Dollie on the dance floor. Others would always have to take his place at her side. After just one slow dance, his hip ached miserably and the ball of his foot was sore.

He raised his glass again and took another gulp of whiskey.

I've got to get out of here.

He lifted himself scraping the chair on the floor as he scooted it backwards. The dance ended and Dollie headed his way. Yates swallowed the gall in his throat just as the horns tooted the introduction to another fast song.

"Can't you dance with me Yates?" Dollie smiled and took his hand.

"You go ahead without me, Dollie. I need some

fresh air." He pulled his hand from hers and walked away calling over his shoulder. "I'll be back for you later."

Dollie's shoulders sagged. "Where you going?"

He shrugged.

Dollie watched Yates limp toward the door. Her face mirrored her disappointment. Lately, more times than not, he left her at the club coming back hours later with no explanation for where he'd been. Tears glistened in her eyes.

Whirling around Dollie stood face to face with Butch. He grabbed her hands and led her back onto the floor. She jerked her hands back and quickly wiped her tears, placed her hands back in his, took a deep breath and threw herself into dancing the Charleston. Across the room Yates paused at the door, turning just in time to see Dollie throw her head back in joyous laughter, her arms and legs swinging gaily in time to the music.

Outside, Yates cranked his truck and drove away. Let Dollie have her fun, he had work to do. Real work. A man's work.

Much later that night, he made his way back to the club. Dollie looked as if she had not even paused in her dancing. She waved her hand to him and started in on the next dance. Yates sat again at the table watching and toying with his drink. Sweat poured from his forehead.

The dance ended and Dollie floated out to the truck as if walking on clouds. Yates staggered behind her.

"Had a good time, didn't you, Doll?" Yates lips curled in a snarl as he opened the vehicle door for her, "Dancing with Butch all night." He spit out the words.

Dollie's face fell, the corners of her mouth drooping. "You should have stayed and danced with me."

On the ride home the air was thick with silent disappointment. Dollie leaned back and drew a heavy breath. "Where do you go, Yates, when you leave me at the club?"

"Taking care of business."

"What business?"

Yates turned his head to look at her. The car swerved.

"Watch out, Yates!" she cried, "You'll wreck us."

"No I won't," he shot back.

Angry tears rose to Dollie's eyes. "You promised me you'd quit."

"Quit what?" he growled.

"You know good and well what I'm talking about," she snapped. "Don't play dumb with me."

"Are you calling me dumb, Little Doll?" he said, his voice edged with sarcasm.

Dollie let out a long sigh. "I hate when you're drunk."

"Hate? You hate? Well. I hate when you spend half the night in the arms of another man."

"What? I'm only dancing!"

"Dancing, my foot! I see you out there with Butch's hands all over you."

"Why, Yates! You're jealous. How could you be! You know he means nothing to me." Dollie's lips puckered in a pout. "I just like to dance and you're never around." She crossed her arms over her middle and looked out the window.

They pulled up at the Carter's home. Yates went in and brought Norma out. As soon as they were in their own house, Dollie tucked Norma in bed, made sure she was asleep then tread back to the bedroom.

"You promised me you'd quit," Dollie said with fire in her eyes.

"I know, Dollie and I will." Yates voice was subdued now.

She stomped her foot. "When, Yates? When?"

Yates sat on the side of the bed and began to sweet talk her, "Aw', I don't want to fuss anymore. Let's make up. Come to bed with me, Doll" As he reached to pull her to him, Dollie saw something bright red on his collar.

She gasped. "You've been with somebody else!"

"What are you talking about now?" he mumbled.

"I'm talking about lipstick on your shirt," she said through clenched teeth.

"Aw, that? It's nothing."

"Nothing! Nothing!" She screeched. "How dare you say, it's nothing!"

"So men can have their hands all over you at the club, but I can't have one little hug?"

Fire flashed in Dollie's eyes and Yates quickly added, "It really was nothing, Dollie. A woman tripped and fell on my shoulder at the bar, that's all."

"Liar!" Dollie slapped his face so hard he saw stars.

Yates fell back on the bed.

Dollie ran to the kitchen for ice to nurse her stinging hand. When she returned to the bedroom, Yates lay in the same spot with his clothes still on. Fast asleep.

The next morning, he put on his work clothes, tiptoed out of the house and left for the job without waking Dollie, knowing he had to face her after work. That was too soon. Sure enough, that evening she stood waiting for him in the living room.

Her bag was packed.

Thinking he could smooth things over, he said, "What are you doing with a suitcase, Dollie?"

"Norma and I are going to Mama's. If you ever want us back you can quit drinking and come get us. I won't live like this."

The color blanched from his face. He swallowed hard. "You don't mean that, Dollie." He tried to take her in his arms.

She pushed him away. "Drop us off at Mama's house. You can keep the truck for work." Her words came out in clipped tones.

"Wait, Dollie. Don't do this," he pleaded.

She shook her head and stared past him, her eyes blazing.

Yates saw the determined set of her jaw. Her mind was made up. She wouldn't change it no matter what he said. Closing his mouth, his lips formed a straight line.

He picked up the suitcase.

Dollie called to Norma and they left.

Yates heart was in his throat, his mouth dry. He didn't think he could live without Dollie, but he didn't think he could live without his bottle either. He had a choice to make and it wouldn't be easy.

Arriving at the Carter home, Dollie and Norma got out. Yates carried her suitcase to the porch as Mama Carter opened the door. She eyed the suitcase.

"What's this, Dollie?"

"Mama, do you mind if Norma and I stay with you for a few days? I haven't been feeling well."

"Is anything wrong between you and Yates?"

Dollie looked at Yates. He hung his head. "Nothing we can't work out," he said.

"Well, that's good. I'd hate to see anything split up the two of you."

"Yates works long hours and he's gone most evenings. At least you'll be here at night."

"Come on in Dollie. You know you can stay as long as you need to . . . that is if Yates is in agreement to it."

Yates nodded and left with, "I'll see you in a few days, Dollie."

Trying to sound more cheerful than she felt she said, "Okay."

The house was quiet when Yates got home, too quiet. He didn't want to go to a Klan meeting; he wanted his wife and daughter. Opening a cabinet door he uncovered his bottle. His hand shook as he grabbed it out and set it on the table.

No! He couldn't, he wouldn't.

He set the bottle back in the cabinet with a thud and walked through the empty house. Dollie's mark was in the bedroom, where the light green chenille bedspread lay neatly smoothed, the wood floors swept clean with dark green throw rugs beside the bed.. Opening the closet Yates laid his face against Dollie's favorite red dress. The faint scent of her perfume brought a fresh wave of longing for her.

He shuffled back to the kitchen, pulled out the frying pan and scrambled an egg. The egg stuck in his throat. That wasn't what he wanted. He could almost see the bottle through the closed cabinet. Before he realized what was happening his hand opened the door, reached for the bottle and turned it up to his mouth.

Arriving home from work the next day the house seemed quieter than before. When he entered the door, Yates missed the pitter-patter of Norma's little feet as she ran to meet him grabbing him around the legs in a childish hug.

He looked into the kitchen, but Dollie wasn't standing at the stove cooking supper and humming as she stirred a pot of grits. He missed sneaking up behind to hug her as she stood there frying fish. He missed hearing her gasp and say, "Oh, Yates! You scared me." Then smile at him and say, "Supper's almost done." He missed the tantalizing aroma when she opened the oven door to remove a pan of homemade biscuits or cornbread.

He tried to brush the thoughts aside, made a sardine and onion sandwich and washed it down with a cup of hot coffee. He remembered how Dollie hated when he opened a can of the highly scented fish. Lately the offensive odor made her gag and run to throw up.

He went to an empty bed and felt the smooth cloth over the pillow where Dollie usually laid her head. He tried to doze, but sleep evaded him with Dollie's warm body missing. One thought after another ran through his head, thoughts of good times. Finally, he got up and went back to the kitchen. His bottle waited right where he left it. He yanked it out of the cabinet, looked at the label, and then put it back. Guilt flooded him as he grabbed it again, turned it up and took a long swig.

Yates tossed and turned most of the night, dreaming that Dollie continually slipped from his arms. When morning came, he got out of bed so tired he could hardly hobble across the floor. His hip hurt. The house echoed from emptiness. How would he make it without his Doll?

A cup of Cuban coffee would at least give him energy. He headed for a Cuban Restaurant in Ybor City where crowds of people shouted across the room to each other in Spanish. He often stopped there to visit and get a caffeine pick-me- up.

Several of the Klansmen he knew ate there. Talking to them might ease his loneliness. Soon one of the gang members, George Wolfson, sat across from him at the breakfast table. After a few minutes of shoveling food into his mouth, George glanced around the restaurant and said in a low voice, "Where were you last night, Kidd?"

Yates swallowed his coffee in a loud gulp. "My wife had a little problem."

George's eyes shifted. He leaned toward Yates. "Had to get Harvey to take your place. That don't look good."

"I know, but what could I do?" Yates protested. "Can't let her get suspicious, can I?"

George nodded.

"How'd it go? Get the job done?" Yates whispered.

"Yeah. We sure could' a used your help on this one, though."

For a second, Yates looked away.

George continued so softly Yates had to strain to

hear him. "We had a tip that Andy Smith, the next guy on the list, would be at a bar on Nebraska Avenue. We got lucky. Soon as we swung over, there he was walking down the sidewalk."

Yates leaned forward his mouth dry. "What happened?"

"Well, Harvey jumped out and slick as a whistle put a gun in Andy's ribs. Told him, 'get in the car, Smith . . . taking you for a little ride.'"

"Any trouble?"

"Yeah. I had to get out and help."

"Did ya . . .?" Yates whispered, faltering a bit.

"Kill him?" George finished for Yates. He nodded. "One bullet to the head," George smirked. A devilish look passed across his face. "Then we took off for the Hillsborough."

Sweat popped out on Yates forehead. "Another one, huh?"

George nodded again. "Another one."

Yates remembered an incident a few weeks earlier when he approached the Hillsborough River Bridge. Flashing lights from cop cars and a crowd of people gathered around the bridge blocked traffic. Yates stopped and walked toward the commotion to see what had happened. A body floated in the water face down. The only visible parts were head and arms. He watched as rescuers dragged out the bloated corpse. A rope hung loose from one ankle where a cement block came unattached. Yates held his breath and watched them cut the remaining block loose and turn the corpse over. Yates gasped. In spite of the swelling he recognized Ben Crane – another name on the list.

George studied Yates for a moment. His eyes darkened and he frowned.

"How come you're never there, Kidd . . . When the deal is done?"

Yates hung his head. "I don't know . . . Something always happens." He looked up and added, "Last time with Crane," he whispered, "I got called back to work."

"Yeah, yeah," George mumbled. With a fierce look he pointed his finger at Yates and said, "You need to be there, Kidd."

Yates nodded. "I'll be there next time."

George rose, dug his money out of his pocket, paid his bill and headed for the door. Turning back, he looked at Yates and said, "See you around, Kidd . . . next time." He stuck his hat on his head and walked out.

Yates wiped his forehead on the napkin, paid his bill and left for work. Alone in the truck his stomach churned as he thought about the killings. Each time he was supposed to help, his Mama's prayers played over and over in his head. Haunted him. So far, he was unable to force himself to go and participate. Feeling so much less than the man he wanted to be, he picked up his whiskey bottle lying in the seat beside him and took a long swig. He didn't worry about it anymore.

Twenty-five

The house was emptier than ever when Yates went home that night. Solitude enveloped him like a gray mist covers a ship on a foggy night. It felt like his right arm was cut off. He hated being alone and wondered if Dollie missed him.

When he finally did get to sleep, he dreamed about her again. In this dream a cross burned. When Dollie tried to put it out, her clothes caught fire. Yates grabbed her and rolled her in the dirt to extinguish it, but when he put out his hand to help her up, she was gone. Instead a horse arose and galloped away.

Yates sprung up in the bed, his clothes wet with perspiration. He had to see her and know that she was all right before it was too late.

In his mind, he saw every detail of her face: her cute smile with the space between her two front teeth, her tiny nose, her velvety skin and most of all her beautiful soft brown eyes – the eyes that flashed, glistened, and revealed her moods. He loved her laugh, her cry, and the way she talked playfully when she was happy. He smelled a lingering scent of her perfume on the sheets. He remembered her tender touch on his face, the sting of her angry slap, and the passionate way she made love. Never sure of her reactions, Yates thought life with Dollie was exciting. He wanted her. She said to come for her when he was ready.

A battle of questions raged in his mind. Was he ready? Could he quit drinking? Dollie demanding that he give up whiskey was unfair. He hadn't asked her to stop dancing. *I'll give her one more day and see if she changes her mind.*

That night, before Yates went to another cross-burning, he had to have a drink. So what if he drank, and stayed out late with the Klan? It was his duty to help with the beatings and cross-burnings to protect his wife, his family and his country, but he needed a drink first. Why couldn't Dollie see that?

Late in the night, alone in bed, he faced the question he avoided earlier – which one meant the most to him, Dollie or whiskey? It was as simple as that. He had promised to quit, but was he willing? He battled on and on through the night. Finally, before daylight, he knew his answer.

That evening after work, Yates headed the truck in the direction of the Carter's house. His mouth was dry when he knocked quietly on the door and heard light footsteps. Norma ran, swung the door open and sailed into his arms.

"Daddy, Daddy," she said with her arms around his neck hanging on for dear life. "Mama's been crying for you."

He hugged her tightly then set her down when Dollie appeared looking sheepish.

"Come on in, Yates." She opened the screen.

Yates stepped inside. He wanted to grab her in his

arms, hold her and never let go, but pride wouldn't let him. She had left him.

"How are you, Dollie?" he said gently.

"Not too good." Her tone was soft, subdued. "I got some news from the doctor yesterday."

"What news?"

"I'm pregnant again."

"Aw, honey, that's great." He smiled and reached for her.

She hesitated. "He thinks there might be complications this time." Tears welled in her eyes. "I'm scared, Yates. I want to come home."

She stepped toward him. He opened his arms wide. She fell into them. He held her tight as Norma grabbed them around their legs.

"I have to be honest with you, Dollie."

"About what?"

"I haven't been able to quit the booze yet."

"You will."

Daddy Carter came in the back door and walked straight through to the living room. He shook Yates' hand and smiled. "Congratulations, Yates. You may get that boy you wanted, after all."

"Yeah," Yates nodded and grinned.

"Doll hasn't felt well. It's a good thing you brought her over here so Janie could help her at night with Norma."

"I've been pretty busy lately." Yates looked down.

"Norma's been coughing a lot," Daddy Carter continued. "Ought' a let the doctor check her, Yates."

"She'll be all right, Daddy." Dollie pulled Norma to her. "I'll take care of her."

Mama Carter came in. "Yates!" she said putting her purse on the table. "Stay for supper. It won't take long to cook."

Yates longed for a good home cooked meal. "Thanks, I will." He picked up Norma, held her on one arm and put the other one around Dollie. They were a family again.

Mama Carter hustled to the kitchen, Dollie right behind her. Soon Yates heard pots and pans rattling and before he and Daddy Carter finished listening to the news on the radio at WDAE, the appetizing aroma from a platter of fried chicken and steaming bowls of potatoes and green beans drew them to the supper table.

That night, with Dollie and Norma back home, Yates felt complete again. Nobody, not even Janie Carter, as much as he enjoyed her cooking, could fix a better meal than his Doll, and to think that she was going to give him another child. Life was good. He would quit drinking for Dollie and his family. He owed it to them.

This pregnancy was different. Dollie cramped and spotted frequently. The doctor advised her to stay off her feet. It was hard with a two-year-old underfoot. Dell came every few days with her son Tommy, who was a couple of years older than Norma. They played together. Dell helped Dollie with housework and cooking. Mama Carter dropped in several afternoons a week after she got home from work, most of the time with supper.

Yates told himself every day that he would cut back on drinking, come home earlier and help, but he didn't.

One day, during Dollie's resting time, she suddenly

realized that Norma was quiet – too quiet. Getting off the bed she walked through the house. Near the living room door she saw her yellow wooden duck that held her scissors – empty. A trail of water led to Norma hiding behind the door. She sat with the gold fish bowl between her knees, the scissors in one little hand, and a gold fish in the other. The fish's fins lay on the floor.

Dollie gasped and burst into tears when she saw a huge gap in Norma's hair just above her forehead.

"What are you doing? Give me those scissors and go sit on the couch, young lady, right now!"

Norma obeyed, but looked hard at her mother then cocked her head to the side and asked, "Mommy, why you cry?"

"Just look at your hair!" Dollie sobbed.

When Yates walked in the door after work and saw Dollie's eyes, red and swollen, he knew something was wrong.

"What's the matter?" he asked.

"It's hard to watch Norma every minute of the day and rest, too." She gave him a fiery look, "Especially when I can think of nothing else but you still staying out half the night drinking!"

"I know Dollie. I *am* going to quit."

"It's about time you stopped talking and did it!"

"I will. Is that what you've been crying about?"

"No. Norma got a hold of my scissors."

"And?"

"Go look at her!"

Yates walked into the living room where Norma sat on the couch, her arms folded. He spotted the gap.

"What in the world happened to your hair?"

She smiled sweetly, "I give 'e haircut." She patted the top of her head. Grinning impishly she shrugged her shoulders and pointed to the bowl on the coffee table where the goldfish floated, finless.

"What happened to the fish?" Yates said solemnly.

"I give 'e haircut, too," she said clapping her hands.

He turned away quickly to hide the smile he found impossible to control. Scolding would have to come later.

The next day Yates and Dollie took Norma to the beauty parlor. The beautician cut off all of her hair so it would grow out evenly. She looked just like a little boy. Dollie cried again.

The scissors incident was the big discussion at Mama Carter's next family dinner. Dollie told the story with great expression, her voice rose and fell as she waved her hands for emphasis. The adults broke into laughter including Dollie. Yates chuckled proud that she was such a fine mother, after all. He couldn't wait for the next little bundle to arrive.

One night when Dollie was about five months along, Yates went to a Klan beating and afterwards drank too much. He came home later than usual, his clothes wet with sweat, his hair rumpled. Tiptoeing in, he hoped Dollie was asleep. Instead, she sat in bed propped against her pillows, rubbing her stomach and moaning.

"What's wrong, Dollie?"

"Oh, Yates, I thought you'd never get here. My stomach's hurting real bad, like it did when Norma was born."

"It's too early for that."

"I know. You'd better get the doctor and see if Mama can come."

Yates rushed out to the truck feeling weak in the knees. He woke Dr. Dyer and circled by to get Mama Carter.

When they got to the house, before he reached the porch, Yates heard Dollie crying out in agony. Mama Carter dashed through the door and assisted the doctor. Yates hung back dreading to go inside. Finally he made his way into the house, paced back and forth drinking black coffee, feeling helpless and ashamed. He heard Dollie groaning and struggling, but was unable to make himself go into the room.

When Dollie quieted down at last, Yates gathered his nerve and eased inside. Dollie lay on the bed still and grim. Water gathered in her eyes and shimmered in the lamp light.

Yates looked toward the doctor and glimpsed something in his hand. He strode to his side and saw lying in Dr. Dyers palm a tiny lifeless form – a baby boy.

Yates fell to his knees beside the bed and laid his head next to Dollie. Trying to hold back the tears of remorse and anguish, he bit his lip. He felt as if his heart would burst. He shook with grief. Finally he let go and sobbed long mournful wails. When he hushed Dollie put her hand on his head. He lifted his face and saw tears rolled down her cheeks.

"I lost your son," she whispered.

He slowly shook his head. "I should have been here."

Mama Carter wept softly behind him. When they all gained their composure, she said. "Don't either one of you blame yourselves. These things just happen."

The doctor agreed. "It's nobody's fault," he said and turned away, but not before Yates saw tears in his eyes, too.

Much of that sleepless night, Yates walked the floor and chain-smoked his Chesterfields. The son he had longed for was dead.

Tomorrow we will bury him, and with him, my dreams. As surely as I live and breathe, I killed my son.

Twenty-six

For days, Yates walked in a dark cloud, unable to shake the feeling of despair and loneliness that surrounded him like a shroud. Everywhere he turned he saw the small lifeless body of his son as it lay in Doctor Dyer's hand – a perfect infant, but without the breath of life.

One Saturday morning he walked out on his front porch attempting to clear his mind. Earl, a good friend and member of the Klan, lived across the street with his father and mother. Yates sat in the quiet of the morning and looked toward the house as Earl walked out on his front porch. In one hand he held a shot glass, in the other a lemon. Stopping at the porch railing, he gazed up into the summer sky.

What in the world is Earl up to? Yates watched as Earl put the glass to his lips, drank the liquid, sucked the lemon, then turned and walked back into the house letting the screen door bang behind him.

"Oh, my God, my God!" Yates heard the words before he saw the screen door fly open and Earl's mother burst through, wringing her hands.

"Earl's drunk strychnine!" she screamed.

Darting across the street, Yates bounded up the steps and rushed inside. "Earl, what's the matter with you?

Why did you go and do a thing like that?"

"Leave me alone. I *want* to die."

"Why?"

"My life's a mess, Kidd. You wouldn't understand."

"Try me."

He shook his head.

Yates tried to talk sense into him but hardly knew what to say. What do you say to a dying man? Earl's mama called the ambulance. Within fifteen to twenty minutes, the wail of the siren drowned out the rest of Yates words.

Tom, a Klan member, drove the ambulance. Fred, another Klansman, rode in the back. They hurried inside with a stretcher and put Earl on it.

"We're gonna get you to the hospital, Earl." Fred threw a sheet over him.

Suddenly, like a wild man Earl began to fight the sheet, kicking and screaming.

"Get this thing off of me!" he yelled and pulled his legs up higher in the stretcher. "Can't you see those flames around my feet? They're burning me!" His eyes held a look of terror. "Get me out of these flames, Fred." He looked at Yates. "Kidd, help Fred pull me out of the flames. I can't stand it!"

Yates tried to convince him. "There are no flames, Earl."

"Yes, there is! Don't you see 'em coming up my body? I can't stand the heat. Pull me out!"

"We'll get you help." Tom and Fred loaded him into the back of the ambulance.

Yates stood watching – helpless.

Before Tom shut the door, Earl looked him squarely in the eyes and said, "Tom, if you've ever driven an ambulance, drive this one! I thought I wanted to die, but I see I ain't ready to meet God!"

All the way to the hospital Earl screamed "Don't let me die! I can't stand the flames!"

Just as they approached the emergency room doors, Earl took his last breath.

* * *

When Fred came back to tell Yates, he hung his head and fought back tears. Yates and Earl had both tried to make people do the right thing by beating them and burning crosses, yet Earl ended his own life regardless of his work with the Klan.

Yates realized that he, too, needed more than the Klan.

That night in bed, Yates turned and tossed and heard Earl's words again and again, "Get me out of these flames." Over and over Yates saw Earl try to pull his feet up out of the fire.

The preacher's voice from the tabernacle years ago rang in Yates ears. "Alcohol will damn your soul to a devil's hell where the fire is not quenched. You'll burn forever."

Yates wondered if Earl was burning in hell. Had he seen himself sliding into the pit of hell fire, or was he hallucinating and burning from strychnine? Yates had heard that people feel hot when they ingest it, but he had never heard of them seeing flames or saying that they were not ready to meet God.

Yates thought about his closest associates. One by

one they had fallen. Several were in prison for life. Various ones died from accidents, some were shot, and now Earl – suicide. Yates felt as if death were claiming all his friends. Would he be next? Sweat popped out on his forehead. He didn't want to take a chance on meeting God. Not now.

He was as unprepared as Earl.

Footnote: After ingesting strychnine, a person's consciousness or thinking are not affected at first (except that the person is very excitable and in pain). Eventually the muscles tire and the person can't breathe. Symptoms of poisoning usually appear within 15 to 60 minutes. High doses cause symptoms within 15 to 30 minutes: Respiratory failure, (inability to breath) possibly leading to death, brain death.
Most direct symptoms are violent convulsions.

Kidd
and
Dollie

Changed

1934-1939

Twenty-seven

Yates was eating his breakfast when Dollie called frantically, "Yates, come here! Something's wrong with Norma!"

He pushed his grits and eggs aside. With fresh memories of his baby boy's death and Earl's suicide, he hurried into the bedroom.

Little two and a half-year-old Norma lay coughing and gasping for breath. With no time to waste they rushed her to the doctor. Immediately, he admitted her to the Hospital.

Lying in a child's white iron bed that resembled a box with metal slats around it, she looked so fragile. The doctor diagnosed asthma and started medication. Yates had to leave because hospital regulations said that no one was allowed to stay more than fifteen minutes except Norma's mother. In between coughing and fighting to breathe, she begged her daddy not to leave. He felt as if someone stabbed his heart when he walked out of that room. She was his baby, his *only* baby.

Yates went as much as visiting hours and his job permitted, but knew that Dollie made sure the doctors and nurses provided good care for her when he was gone. As soon as the medicine took effect, the doctor said she could have other visitors. Mama and Daddy Carter were among the first. They stayed while Dollie went home for a bath and change of clothes.

Norma was delighted to see them. She climbed to the side of the crib and held out her little trembling hands. "Take me to 'or house," she begged.

"The doctor won't let you go yet," Mama Carter said bending to give her a hug.

"But, I need one of 'or cold bi'kits," she begged.

"I'll bring you a biscuit when you get home."

Norma puckered up and cried while tears of sympathy rolled down Mama Carter's face as she realized Norma was too young to understand why her grandmother wouldn't take her now and give her a biscuit.

At the end of the week, the doctor pronounced her recovered. Yates and Dollie happily took Norma home. However, in the night she grew sick again and the next morning once more gasped for breath.

"Look Mama!" she wheezed. "Angels!" Her small finger pointed to the upper part of the wall.

Yates heard her excited little voice and thought the angels had come for Norma. He didn't know what to do. He had to get out of there. He couldn't watch another one of his children die.

"I've got to go to work, Dollie. Send for me if she gets worse."

Yates saw fear in Dollie's eyes. "I'll stop and tell Dell to check on you after a while," he said giving her a tight, frantic hug.

He kissed Norma on the forehead, limped across the room and eased the door shut. He climbed into his truck and drove away feeling sad and worried. But as he chugged down the road, he noticed how brightly the sun shone. Little by little the sun's warmth began to melt his anxiety the way it melts an icicle hanging from the eves of a house on a northern winter day – drip by drip. *Surely, nothing will go wrong on a beautiful day like this.*

Suddenly the view from the left window of his truck erased all thoughts of Norma. An ordinary sight, just a simple landscape that he had seen many times before, caught his attention, today, in a new way.

On the countryside sprawled a massive oak tree. Graceful swatches of Spanish moss hung from its branches and swayed, silent in a gentle breeze. Deep green grass surrounding the tree provided a vivid contrast to the azure sky. A fluffy white cloud stood out against the deep blue of the sky and formed a backdrop for a dark winged bird that floated along at the same rate of speed as his truck. The open vehicle window created a perfect frame for this masterpiece as the awesome panorama, one lovelier than Yates could ever remember, drifted slowly by his truck

"What a beautiful picture!" he said. Suddenly he became aware of a presence.

Behind every picture there is an intelligent being. He heard the voice from somewhere deep within.

Yes. He agreed and realized that nothing happens on its own. A being designs and creates everything. Pictures do not appear without assistance. An artist paints them.

The voice asked, *who is the intelligent being behind this picture that you see?*

He sucked in his breath. "God!" he said then added softly, "there must be a God!"

If you believe there is a God, who are you that you are not serving Him?

"Yes, who am I that I am not serving God?" He asked himself aloud.

He looked to his right and there in the seat beside him laid his whiskey bottle. It was his constant companion and occupied that spot in the truck wherever he went. It was also the source of contention between him and Dollie, and the reason he was not home in time to help Dollie when she lost his baby son. If he would have been there instead of out drinking maybe the baby would still be inside growing to full term. In an instant, his eyes opened. He saw and understood what else whiskey was – a hindrance to serving God. He picked up the bottle, looked at it and said aloud, "I don't need *you* anymore!"

With all his might, he slung the bottle out of the window. "I'll never drink another drop!"

As the bottle left his hand, the desire to drink flew out with it. A habit that lurked like a shadow in his life disappeared through that truck window and an immense sense of release flooded over Yates. From that day, he could not stand the smell or taste and never again drank another alcoholic beverage.

Yates completed his day's work with a lighter heart and new feelings. He had not surrendered his life completely to God, but he had taken the first step – a start. When he arrived home Dollie met him at the door, crying.

He took her in his arms and looked around for Norma. She sat in the floor playing quietly and breathing normally. "What's wrong, Dollie?"

"I don't know, Yates. This has been the strangest

day." She paused to wipe her eyes and finally gained her composure. "You know, Yates, I have been thinking all day that we need to go to church. When Norma was so sick this morning, she saw angels. We need to take her to church."

"This was a strange day for me too, and I've been thinking along those same lines," Yates said.

Dollie's lips quivered. "Today, I knelt down beside the couch where Norma lay and tried to pray, but I didn't know how, Yates." Her soft brown eyes were pleading as she said, "Do you know how?"

"No," he said in a whisper.

"Maybe they'll teach us at church."

"Yeah." He gave her another squeeze not yet ready to talk about his own experience that day. Wrinkling his nose toward the scent coming from the kitchen, he sniffed. "Do I smell roast beef cooking?"

"Oh, Yates, all you think about is something to eat." She wiped away the last of her tears and gave him a tiny smile. "No, it's meatloaf and mashed potatoes."

"That'll do!"

Dollie had already set the plates and silverware on the table. Glasses filled with ice waited on the kitchen counter. She went to the oven, carefully took out the meatloaf and set it on hot pads in the middle of the table. After pouring steaming vegetables into bowls, she placed them on each side of the meat, then went back to pour sweet tea into the frosty glasses.

Yates carried Norma to the sink and helped her wash her hands then eased her into her wooden highchair.

"I'm so worried about her," Dollie said tilting her head toward Norma as she sat down in her chair.

Yates nodded. "Me, too."

Dollie dipped a plate of food for Norma and set it aside to cool before she settled it on the highchair tray. "You know, Yates," she continued, "I didn't go to church much growing up, but we just *have* to start going."

"I know, Dollie, and we will."

"When?"

"This Sunday."

Dollie sighed. "I hope so." She looked wistfully at Yates.

When they finished eating, Dollie quickly cleared the table while Yates wiped Norma's face and hands then lifted her from the chair. He kissed the top of her head before setting her on the floor to play.

The couple was silent while Dollie washed the dishes in hot sudsy water and Yates dried and put them away. The only sound was the rattle of the dishes.

Outside, the late evening sun hid behind black clouds as rain poured from the sky. Inside, the sound of thunder and torrential rain along with the smell of wet dirt dampened Dollie's spirit even more. The couple headed for bed earlier than usual but neither one could settle down and sleep.

Yates had said they would go to church Sunday, but Dollie couldn't wait until then. It was impossible to haul around this weight much longer, the weight that pushed her down, smothered her. She must have relief from the awful feelings of condemnation and guilt, now. Dollie blew out a long sigh. "Pray for me, Yates," she said.

"I can't pray for you, Dollie," he answered. "I need somebody to pray for me."

Desperate for help, Dolly wailed, "Oh God!"

That was her complete prayer. She cried it loud enough for the neighbors to hear. Those two words, propelled from the bottom of her heart, voiced her longing to know God, articulated her desire for a different life, a new one.

"Yates, there's a light in the corner of the room," she whispered. "Do you see it?"

"No," he said, "But I feel something."

"Oh, Yates, I do, too. It feels like somebody just took a big load off of me. It's gone! I feel light as a feather."

The rain had stopped outside the house while inside Dollie laughed, cried, held up her hands, and thanked God. She told Yates the next morning that all night she floated on the bed in the light of God's presence and experienced a glorious sense of peace. In an instant, and through that two-word prayer, Dollie's life started to change.

Yates believed she experienced the same God that night whom he met on the highway that day, but he still wasn't ready to tell her about his experience. Although he took a step in the right direction, he hadn't made a full commitment to God. He wasn't ready, yet, to give up certain things.

Twenty-eight

Early Sunday morning, Dollie dressed Norma and herself while Yates put on his best clothes. He planned to attend a church across town, but as they approached the Buffalo Avenue Church of God, a strange thing happened. It felt like someone else's hands took the steering wheel from him and turned the truck into the parking lot. He passed that church daily for a year on his truck route, but had never seen it.

Hiding his surprise, he told Dollie, "I think we'll go here." He parked the truck and the three walked inside. Feeling timid and unsure, Yates guided Dollie and Norma to a seat on the back row.

A tall man wearing a suit and a huge smile came and extended his hand to Yates. As they shook hands, Yates noticed his grip was firm and strong.

"My name is Jake Roberts. I'm the pastor. We sure are glad to have you folks with us today."

Right away Yates liked this man and believed he meant what he said, that he really was glad to have them in church. Several other people followed him and greeted the family warmly. Yates and Dollie felt love like they had never experienced flowing from these people and realized they were starving for that kind of love.

"I like it here," Yates whispered to Dollie.

"Me, too," she answered.

Just before the service started another man introduced himself and said, "It's good to see you in church today."

"Glad to be here." Yates shook his hand. "I'm Yates Kidd. This is my wife, Dollie, and the little one is Norma."

The man nodded. "Do you live in the area?"

"Yes, we do." Yates answered. "Over in Jackson Heights."

"Well, of all things. You live on 24ᵗʰ Avenue, don't you?"

"How did you know?"

"I'm your mailman, I recognized your name." He shook his head. "This is great . . . just great . . . I have been praying for God to save someone on your block and bring them to this church." He took out a handkerchief and wiped his eyes. "God sure is faithful to answer prayer."

A little shiver went down Yates spine. To think this man prayed for them as he delivered letters to their house. *No wonder the car seemed bent on turning in at this church.* Dollie's mouth dropped open and her eyes widened. She looked as surprised as Yates felt.

As the service started, people gathered up front and formed a choir. When they sang and clapped their hands to the beat of the music, their faces glowed as if a light from another world shone on them. They swayed and patted their feet on the wooden floor. One woman twirled around and around on her toes, her face radiant with joy. As their enthusiastic voices rang out over the congregation, goose bumps ran up Yates arms. He thought of the tabernacle services he attended as a boy and the first miracle he witnessed – his Daddy's healing. He remembered his Mama being baptized in the Holy Ghost and knew without a doubt that what these people had was real.

Yates looked at Dollie. She had such a look of longing on her face. She glanced back at him, smiled, and pulled Norma closer to her.

Pastor Jake Roberts preached a good sermon, but Yates struggled to concentrate on what he said. The presence he felt a few days ago was back and enveloped him, the same presence he felt as a boy and tried to wipe out of his life with drinking and carousing in sin. It was a presence he longed to experience anew.

As he neared the end of his sermon, the pastor's words grabbed Yates' attention. They described him. He felt like Jake Roberts had taken a paint brush and painted a picture of Yates' life, sins and all, and hung it up for everyone to see. Yates wondered who told the preacher about him.

When he finished, Brother Roberts, as they called him, gave an invitation to come forward if you wanted to know God. Dollie almost ran to the front. Yates hung back with the excuse that he needed to tend to Norma. While he watched, Dollie knelt at a curved wooden altar. Several ladies gathered around her to pray.

"What do you want from God?" Monnie McClure asked her. Monnie was a tall thin spinster with long braids of hair that crossed on top of her head.

"I want whatever you people have. You look so happy. I want what makes you happy."

"Well, it's Jesus and the Holy Ghost," Monnie said.

"Then that's what I want."

"First you have to ask Jesus to forgive you of your sins."

"Jesus, forgive me of my sins," Dollie cried out in a loud voice. She didn't care who heard her. "Oh, Jesus, please forgive me of my sins," she shouted.

"Ask Him to wash you in His blood," Pastor Robert's wife said. She was an attractive, well-dressed woman about five years older than Dollie. Her dark, curly hair was pulled back and gathered in an invisible hairnet. At the neck of her dress she wore a large broach.

"Jesus, wash me in your blood," Dollie cried at the top of her voice.

Sister Parrish, an older, motherly type woman took her turn to instruct. "Now ask Him to sanctify you," she encouraged.

"Sanctify me, Jesus," Dollie yelled with tears streaming down her face. "Please sanctify me."

On and on they led her down the path of salvation, teaching her words to say that she had never heard before, words that Yates had long forgotten. When the praying stopped one by one, they all hugged her.

"You are one of us now," the pastor's wife said. "You're our sister in the Lord."

"Sister? I'm your sister?" She looked at them, her eyes bright, her face covered in a smile. They all smiled back and nodded. She had a brand new family; one she hadn't known existed.

In the warmth of the happy faces encircled around her, she began to ask questions. "What does it mean to be sanctified?"

"It means to be totally cleaned up from the world and set apart for service," Sister Roberts answered.

"All your past sins are gone, covered with the blood of Jesus," Monnie McClure added.

"And it means you are a candidate for the Holy Ghost," Sister Parrish spoke up.

"What's the Holy Ghost?" Dollie's eyes were open wide. "Does that make you a Holy Roller?" She had heard about them when she was a teenager.

"No," Sister Roberts laughed, a glint of gold sparkled on one of her teeth. "The Holy Ghost is the Spirit of God. When you get baptized in the Holy Ghost, you will speak in tongues like they did on the day of Pentecost. Do you have a Bible?"

"No."

"Get yourself one and read it every day. Start in Matthew. When you get to the book of Acts, you *will* understand about the Holy Ghost. We'll pray for you to get it then. It's a gift."

"You mean there's more than what I got today?"

"Oh, yes, lots more." Sister Roberts face grew somber, her smile gone. "Now, there are some things that you will have to change," she said quietly and began instructing her in the teachings of the church. Among the rules were:

No wearing jewelry or makeup
No dancing or going to night clubs
No drinking or smoking
No chewing gum or drinking coffee
No wearing slacks or skimpy clothing
No belonging to secret organizations

Though some of the rules were extreme, Dollie was eager to do whatever they said. No sacrifice was too big for the blessing she found. She was willing to give up everything to be free of the fear that had tormented her ever since she could remember. She would stand on her head, if that were what it took to keep this new joy and peace.

"And don't forget that you have to come to church every service." Monnie said.

"When do you have services?"

"Sunday morning, Sunday night, Wednesday night and Friday night."

"I'll be here." Dollie returned to her seat with a glow on her face that matched the others.

Yates didn't go forward that Sunday. Though he had stopped drinking, he still hadn't told Dollie about that experience and wondered if she had noticed. For some reason it was easy to put down the whiskey bottle and he didn't even have withdrawals, but to free him-self from other hindrances he feared would be harder. He didn't think he was ready for that kind of change.

It may be easy for Dollie to give up her makeup, jewelry and slacks, he thought, but he had more to lose. What would he do about his membership in the secret organization? He couldn't get out of that. Few men left it and lived. Surely, God would not require that of him. Dollie would not die if she stopped wearing makeup and jewelry as this church taught. Then he remembered how much Dollie loved going to the nightclubs and dancing. If she were willing to give up dancing, maybe, just maybe, there was hope for him.

Then he thought of his Chesterfields. He simply could not quit smoking.

Twenty-nine

The next morning Dollie stood at the dresser brushing her hair. Yates caught his breath when he entered the door and saw her. Her face still glowed from the day before. Even without makeup she looked beautiful.

Dollie turned and caught his look of endearment. She smiled. "I just know that Mama will want what I've found." Her face fairly shone with enthusiasm, her eyes sparkled. "Can we go tell her and Daddy soon as you get home from work today?"

Yates nodded his agreement.

That evening when they pulled up to the Carter's home they saw a familiar car parked in the side yard. Dollie's sister, Dell, and her husband Paul were there. Their young son Tommy played in the grass running in circles. When he saw them he took off inside yelling, "Mama, Aunt Dollie's here." Then he ran back out, grabbed Norma's hand and the two turned around and around until they fell laughing in the thick grass.

Before Dollie knocked, Dell opened the door. "Dollie!" she exclaimed in her usual exuberant manner.

Dollie returned the greeting. "Dell!" she said with a hug pleased that her sister was there to hear the great news.

Drawing back Dell eyed her suspiciously. "What's

wrong, are you sick?"

"No."

Dell continued to look her over. "You don't have on any makeup." Dell put her hands on her hips. "Where's your lipstick?"

Dollie shrugged and smiled. "I don't wear it anymore."

"Why? You look pale without it."

"I went to church yesterday. Dell, it was wonderful . . . what I experienced!"

"I don't know what that has to do with your makeup, but you need to put some on." She glanced at Yates then back to Dollie. "You don't look so good without it. You're going to make Yates want another woman if you don't fix yourself up."

Yates stepped up behind Dollie and put his hands on her shoulders. "That won't happen, Dell. Dollie is beautiful to me the way she is."

Janie came from the kitchen wiping her hands on her apron. "What's all the fuss about?"

Dollie hugged her. "Oh, Mama, I have some great news."

"Yeah," Dell interrupted. "She doesn't wear lipstick anymore."

"Mama, I got saved yesterday!"

"You what?"

"I went to church and got saved!"

Dell's husband Paul slapped his leg and shouted. "Well I'll be damned! Dollie's gone and got religion!"

"Mama, I accepted Jesus as my Lord and Savior." Dollie said ignoring Paul's remark. "It's wonderful! I have a brand new feeling of joy!"

"Where is your makeup, Dollie?"

"They told me at church not to wear it anymore."

Janie looked at Dollie's ears and fingers. "Where's your jewelry?"

"I took it all off."

"Even your wedding band?"

Dollie nodded.

Janie's face tightened into a frown, her lips drawn. "Did you go to one of those Holy Roller churches?"

"Yes! No! I don't know. Oh, Mama it started Saturday night. You know how worried I've been about Norma. I felt so restless and heavy. After I went to bed, I cried out to God for help. It seemed like He came into the room and all the worry left me. Then yesterday at church . . . I've never experienced anything like it! I went up front to the altar and prayed. I can't explain the peace and joy. It's wonderful!"

Janie drew back from Dollie her face still covered with a frown. "Well you don't have to get so excited about it." Her tone was cold and cutting.

Oh, Mama," Dollie gasped and let out her breath in a long sigh, her lips straight, unsmiling. "I thought you would want it, too."

"Well, I don't," her mama said sternly. "Whatever made you think I would go for something like that?"

Dollie winced. Her mother's words stung.

Allen Carter had joined the group and heard most of the conversation. "What you did is nice, Doll," he said kindly. "Nothing wrong with going to church to pray, but I doubt the feeling will last." He patted her shoulder. "I 'spect you'll be back to your old self in a few days."

"Oh Daddy, what I found is great. I'll never give it up for anything in the world."

"Now, Doll, I'm sure you'll go to one of your dances soon and forget all about this new religion."

"No Daddy, I'll never go to another dance as long as I live! What I've found is so much better."

Allen frowned. "We'll have to wait and see about that one, Doll. If you don't go dancing again, we'll all know that something very unusual has happened to you."

"You'll see, Daddy." Dollie said quietly.

Each one shook their head in disbelief at Dollie who took all this in stride, her former anger - gone. Where was the old Spitfire Doll?

Thirty

Yates' friend Bill Townsend married Dollie's friend Mabel. The four still got together occasionally. Mabel asked Dollie why she wasn't going to the dances and Dollie told her about the change God had made in her life. After that Mabel wasn't as friendly. It didn't bother Dollie because her life was filled with her new friends at church.

Yates and Bill saw each other at Klan meetings and remained close friends. One day their conversation turned to money. Both agreed that they needed more than they made on their present jobs. They put their heads together and came up with a plan to start a dry cleaning business.

Yates was excited when he discussed it with Dollie. She grew quiet then asked, "Do you think this is what God wants you to do?"

Yates swallowed. He was glad for the changes in Dollie, but didn't want her to get carried away with it. What did God have to do with starting a business? "I think God wants me to do whatever I can to take care of my family, Dollie."

"Okay, Yates," she said sweetly. "But God can take care of us even when we can't take care of ourselves."

"I know, Dollie. Ma believes that, too." He didn't want to tell her, but he believed that was just the way women thought. A man would do everything for his family himself without depending on God for it.

"Whatever you think you should do is fine with me, Yates. I just don't know if Bill is the right one to start a business with. I was thinking of Brother Roberts' sermon on not being unequally yoked together with unbelievers."

"He was talking about marriage, Dollie. We'll just be business partners." Yates stated firmly.

"Seems to me it would still be important."

"Bill's a good friend and has been for years. We can work together. It'll be all right."

She frowned, tossed her head and said, "Do whatever you think, Yates."

Yates read up on the subject, visited other laundry establishments and gave the information to Bill. Yates had stashed a little money from working extra jobs. He and Bill both invested and they started their business in a little hole in the wall in Oak Park, the section of Tampa where Pa and Ma lived.

Bill wanted to call it, *Townsend's Laundry and Dry Cleaners.*

"Wait a minute," Yates said, "I put up as much money as you and did all the leg work. How does Kidd and Townsend sound?"

Bill shot back, "I had the idea. It should be Townsend and Kidd." They deliberated and finally came to an agreement. The hand painted sign in the window read, *Oak Park Laundry and Dry Cleaners.* They both eyed the words, burst into laughter.

Yates slapped Bill on the shoulder. "I like it."

"Me, too."

They were a team. The next day, they ran a quarter page ad in the Tampa Tribune. *Bring us your soiled laundry. We clean professionally.*

Customers arrived, dirty clothes in hand.

Yates became an expert at removing stains. He learned most fabrics can be washed in water and the right soap. He knew which chemical cleaner to use on each material. Occasionally, he pressed. When he couldn't stand on his leg any longer, he delivered the cleaned clothes to the customer's house.

Yates circle of friends increased as he laughed and joked with the customers both in the building and at the door of their homes. He decided people have enough problems without facing a hateful business owner. Unaware of his gift with people, his friendly disposition helped the business grow.

Yates knew it would be a while before all the hard work paid off in the salary department. Since the laundry was closed on Saturdays, he thought of a plan to bring in extra income to tide him over. He didn't want his family to do without and wouldn't ask God to do something he should do himself.

He put his plan for a second job into action. First he talked to Pa and Ma about helping him.

They both agreed.

Pa helped him build a portable food stand. They took it to Ybor City and set it up on Franklin Street in front of Kress's Five and Ten Cent Store. The location was ideal for the Saturday business Yates had in mind. He knew a crowd came in and out of the dime store all day.

After he made arrangements with the Coca Cola

Company to buy drinks at wholesale price, he went in the hardware store and purchased a big galvanized tub to fill with ice.

Early Saturday morning, Yates went to the fisherman's wharf and bought crabs. At home Ma mixed a batch of stuffing with flavorful spices, peppers and onions. Yates headed for their house glad that Pa had moved his family to town. He helped Ma boil the crabs, pull the meat from the shells and add it to the mixture. They stuffed it into the shells and baked them in the oven. By 10:30 he was on his way to Ybor City.

He put the spicy treats in his cart, limped back and forth behind it and cried, "Hot devil crabs, ten cents a-piece. Come and get 'em."

Drawn by the mouth-watering scent, a crowd gathered. He passed them out, as fast as he snatched one out of the steamer, yanked a dripping bottle of cold Coke from the ice bath in the tub, opened the bottle and made change. When the last crab left his hand, he sighed and told the waiting group, "I'll have more next Saturday."

Yates grinned, waved at his new customers and headed for the house to count his money. He remembered the good business ethics Pa taught him and made sure to set aside the amount of money needed for the next Saturday's supply of food. Then, he took Ma's share of the profit to her. He had extra cash in his pocket for Dollie to buy clothes for their growing daughter. He still had energy for his Klan meeting after Dollie and Norma were in bed. All in all, he thought it was a good plan.

He didn't think God minded him working hard and providing for his family either. It would be less for God to worry about. Dollie may not mind depending on Him, but Yates was reluctant. He wasn't sure if God would let him down again like he did with his leg. Yates would take care of himself and his family. Dollie could trust God if she wanted to.

Thirty-one

Yates attended every service at the church with Dollie and enjoyed each one. He listened to the singing, and never tired of seeing the glowing faces of the choir members, especially now that Dollie sang with them.

She was a different woman, and had given up dancing completely.

So why couldn't he give up cigarettes?

Smoking condemned him. Guilt plagued him in every service. The craving for cigarettes held him fast and wouldn't let go. Throwing away the whiskey bottle was easy compared to crumbling up a pack of cigarettes and never smoking another one. He couldn't do it.

While listening and watching the animated people worship God he wondered why he felt condemned by smoking. Tied to it since he was twelve-years-old lighting a cigarette hadn't bothered him before. Why did it bother him now? His smoking didn't hurt anything or anyone . . . did it?

Pastor Roberts drew Yates attention back to the present as he made his altar appeal. "Come and accept Jesus," he begged. Then he asked those who desired the gift of the Holy Ghost to come and pray. Dollie whispered to Yates, "Will you watch Norma, while I go?" She tilted her head toward the altar.

Yates nodded. He watched Dollie walk down the aisle and kneel. The singing grew more dynamic and the pull from the altar stronger. He had to get out of the building. As usual at this time in the service he grabbed Norma and headed out the door. He could hardly wait to light up a Chesterfield and forget the tug at his heart.

Once outside, he propped up his foot on the trucks back fender, sat Norma across his leg and lit his cigarette. Smoke curled around his and Norma's head like blue fog. He waited for Dollie to finish praying, all the while preparing his excuse for leaving the church. *The three-year-old was restless.*

After stomping out the cigarette, he watched Dollie through the church window. She stood with her hands raised and her face shining. Yates pointed toward the window and said to Norma, "Look at Mama. She looks like an angel."

He put Norma in the truck, slid in on the driver's side and was lighting up again when Pastor Roberts came out the church door and headed straight for the truck. Brother Roberts stopped at the driver's side and looked into the smoke filled cab. A sudden draft of air blew the acrid smoke out the window curling it around the pastor's head like a wreath and covering his face.

Brother Roberts fanned the smoke. "Why don't you come back in?" he said. "Your wife has received the blessing of the Holy Ghost. Don't you want to come in and give your heart to the Lord and receive it, too?"

Yates lowered the cigarette, but the smoke rose, twisted and turned determined to find its way back to the pastor's face. After several attempts to keep the smoke down, and it still reaching the pastor, Yates jammed the cigarette down in the ash tray and snuffed it out.

"Not tonight," he answered.

Pastor Roberts sighed and made his retreat.

Yates wondered if Dollie was finished praying yet. He peered into the church window just in time to see her spring into the air and fall flat on her face.

"Let's check on Mama!" he said grabbing Norma in his arms and making a beeline for the church.

After what seemed like forever, Dollie rose from the floor. She was transformed. The look on her face portrayed an experience that came from another world. Her eyes mirrored pure peace.

Something Yates had not felt in years.

He sat Norma on a bench and took Dollie's hand. "Are you all right?"

"Oh yes, Yates, I'm fine."

"You just landed on your face. You're not hurt?"

"No. I never felt a thing."

"What happened?"

"When I spoke in tongues, I thought I had turned into an angel and could fly," she said laughing. "So, I just lifted my hands and jumped." She shrugged. "I didn't fly," she laughed again, "but it felt like I landed on a feather bed."

Yates took her by the shoulder and examined her face. There was not a mark of any kind on it. He pulled her to him and whispered in her ear, "You looked liked like an angel, too"

"Oh, Yates," her voice bubbled with enthusiasm.

"This is the best I ever felt in my life."

Yates drew her into another tight hug, then grabbing Norma with one hand and Dollie with the other, he led them out to the truck.

Once there, he lit another Chesterfield.

Thirty-two

The next day, all Yates could think about was how the cigarette smoke blew into Brother Roberts face and he was desperately ashamed; but the habit controlled him.

That evening when he sat down to the supper table, it felt as if two people stepped up to him, one on each side.

Give them up, said the presence on his right.

You can't give them up, the voice on his left said.

You must give them up. They have become your God.

You can't give them up, said the enemy. *When you are on the job and riding in the truck alone, all you have to do is reach up to your shirt pocket and pull one out. They are your comforter.*

Give them up, said the other presence, *and I will be your comforter.*

Pushing his dinner plate away untouched, he left the table, climbed into his truck, started the engine and backed out of the drive. As he passed an empty field down the road from his house, Yates grabbed the cigarettes out of his shirt pocket and slung them into the weeds.

"I'll never smoke another one, if it kills me," he said aloud.

For the next three days, he went to work as usual, but didn't eat a bite of food or smoke a cigarette. He felt like he would die.

By the third night, Yates' body jerked uncontrollably. Every nerve was tight under his skin. He tossed and turned as sleep eluded him and every cell cried out for nicotine. He had never wanted anything that badly in his life. Not even alcohol had a grip on him like cigarettes. They *had* become his God. Suddenly he knew he could not serve both God and cigarettes. He wondered how something only four inches long could control a person so completely.

"God help me," he cried, yet God seemed a million miles away.

By the fourth day, he was barely able to get out of bed and dress for work. Finally, he made it to the truck. He had to deliver clothes from the drycleaners to one of his regular customers. Arriving at the house he slowly made his way up the steps, his body weak and his nerves frayed. Yates knocked and waited. No one came to the door. He knocked again, still nothing.

Often people left the door unlocked for the laundry man to deliver their dry cleaning. *I'll just leave the clothes in the house and collect the money later.* He turned the knob and pushed the door open about a foot. Just inside on an end table sat a pack of Chesterfields. Two or three of the cigarettes stuck out of the wrapper pointing at him. Sweat popped out on his forehead and trickled down his face. He wanted to grab the cigarettes and eat the whole pack.

With all his strength and using both hands, he pulled the door shut. Hot tears ran down his checks as he stumbled across the wooden porch and down the steps. He wiped his face with his hands and dragged himself to his truck, fell inside and slumped over the steering wheel, his last ounce of strength drained.

"God," he said, "I told you that I would never smoke another cigarette if it killed me and it feels like I'm going to die. If you want me to live, please, help me."

At that time, Yates believed God looked over the portals of heaven and motioned to a band of angels.

"Come here," He said to them. Yates thought God pointed at him and said, "See that man down there in the yellow laundry truck? Go help him."

Suddenly it felt like the cab of his truck filled with angels. He lifted his head and took a deep breath. Strength poured into his body. The craving for cigarettes left along with the shakes and all symptoms of withdrawal.

"Praise God," he cried and raised both his hands as tears flowed unchecked down his face. From that day on the smell of cigarettes made Yates feel sick.

He never desired or smoked another one.

Thirty-three

Yates enjoyed his work at the cleaners more each week. He whistled as he cleaned clothes or rode in his truck to deliver. He didn't even mind sweeping up at night though sometimes it made his hip ache. His hard work and jolly disposition paid off and customers poured in.

Yates expected an increase in pay soon. He felt good about himself and his two jobs. He was glad they provided enough that Dollie could stay home and take care of Norma. She didn't have to go to an outside job as her mama had always done. He didn't want their child in the care of others. He was thankful for the ideas he had of making money and expected the profits to increase.

From the time they opened Oak Park Laundry and Dry Cleaners, Bill insisted on keeping the books. Yates had learned enough about figures from his Pa that qualified him to do the job, too, but Bill insisted that he had the most education. Although Yates knowledge continued to increase through his love for reading, he consented to let Bill handle the books.

Yates had agreed to take a small salary until the business showed a large margin of profit. Bill said he would too. As the customers increased, Yates took home the same pay, but noticed Bill wearing expensive clothes and riding in a new car.

One day, when Bill was gone on an errand, Yates opened the books and did some figuring on his own. After a few minutes, he slammed the books shut. Bill was cheating him.

When he walked in the door, Yates confronted him. "Bill, I need to talk to you."

"About what?" Irritation edged his voice.

"I just checked the books and I'm not getting my share of the profits. We agreed on fifty/fifty."

"I never said that." Bill's lips curled.

"You certainly did. We shook hands on it."

"Look here, Yates, this is my business. I signed the papers to pay the rent. That makes me the owner."

"But you gave me your word. You said . . . "

"It don't matter what I *said*. You don't have anything in *writing*. I do.

"Then your word means nothing?"

"This is my word . . . you'll get the pay I say."

Yates felt the color leave his face. He balled his fist, but it remained at his side. Evenly and paced he said, "You'll get yourself another slave."

Bill's face looked hard like stone. The two men glared at each other.

Yates turned to leave, but walked back. "I had confidence in you, Bill. Thought you were a real friend. Instead, you turned out to be a crook."

Bill shrugged his shoulders and looked away.

As the door slammed behind Yates, his eyes burned and he choked on a lump in his throat. He felt betrayed and hurt. Lost hours invested in his broken dream were important, but not as important as the loss of a friendship. He knew he could get another job, there was always plenty of work for anyone willing to do it, but a friend was hard to find.

Dollie was right when she didn't want me to go in business with Bill an unbeliever. Am I still an unbeliever too?

Yates wasn't sure where he stood with God. He knew now that there was a God. One who asked a lot of a person: his whiskey, his cigarettes, and now his best friend. Did he want God to take control of his whole life? He didn't know, but he knew one thing: he wanted the assurance of salvation Dollie had.

He intended to get it.

Thirty-four

Tonight is my night! Yates pulled into the church parking lot. He *had* to know where he stood with God. He wouldn't put it off another day. He knew God had delivered him from alcohol and nicotine, but he didn't know if he was saved like Dollie. She had the assurance that he wanted. He had to know.

What the preacher said in his sermon that night didn't register as Yates waited for him to say, "Come to the altar." When he finally said *come,* Yates was ready. He hurried down what seemed like a never ending aisle and knelt. He tried to pray, but nothing happened.

His timid spirit whispered, *don't raise your head or your hands. People are watching. Pray quietly, someone might hear you.*

Pride caused his mind to play tricks. He imagined all of his buddies had come into the church and sat staring at the back of his head. He felt their eyes piercing him.

Pride said, *they are laughing at you. Get up. You look stupid. Don't let them see you like this.*

With his arm on the altar and his forehead leaning on it, he raised enough to peek across the altar and saw the pastor pass in front of him. Yates reached out, grabbed the leg of Brother Roberts' trousers and whispered, "Pray for me, Preacher."

Brother Roberts leaned over, patted Yates on the head and said, "God bless this boy." That was all. He walked on.

Yates mind raced again. *He's not interested in you. He wants to go home. All of the other people want to go home, too. Why don't you get up so they can go?*

Determined to receive his answer Yates fought his timidity and raised his head. He turned to the congregation and said, "You can all go home if you want to. I'll be here until time to go to work in the morning, or else hear from heaven. I have to know my standing with God tonight"

Several people got up from their pew, came to the front and began to pray with him. As Yates prayed, he heard a cash register ring. One time, on a visit with Mr. Pollock at the fish market, he lifted two squabs from the freezer, slipped out without paying and took them home for Dollie to cook. He was a thief.

"Forgive me tonight, God and tomorrow I'll pay for those birds," he promised. Yates had never asked for credit, but here he was asking God to forgive him on credit. He owed a debt and tomorrow he would pay it.

After confessing all of the sins he could remember, Yates raised his hands. Something started to happen inside, something he could feel. Suddenly, he fell backwards and lay on the floor.

It appeared that the ceiling rolled to the side. Way up in the heavens a shaft of light slowly opened until it was as wide as Yates' body. The most beautiful colors one could ever imagine streamed down the dazzling width of light, colors that originated in heaven, colors he had never seen, colors that were illuminated by the glory of God.

In this shaft of light, a form descended. As it got closer to Yates, he recognized the form was in the shape of a dove. He watched the dove float down the colorful light until it landed on his chest. When it lit, it felt like a man's hand had slapped him on the chest. As he watched the dove quivered and went inside of him. Simultaneously his tongue grew thick and he began to speak in another language, one that he had not learned. The joy of the Lord spread through his whole being. He lay there nearly an hour speaking in the heavenly language. Yates had received the baptism of the Holy Ghost.

The load of sin on his conscience left. Peace washed over him. Not only was every evil deed he had ever committed gone, but also timidity and pride. The whole package was blown away by the wind of the Holy Spirit. Yates stood, faced the people that stayed and, not caring what anyone thought, spoke boldly, "Now I know where I stand with God."

He lifted one hand, looked up and made a promise to God, "I will be true."

Little did he know the impact those four words would have on him for the rest of his life. He would hear them echo in his mind many times in years to come. . . I will be true . . . I will be true . . . I will be true . . . They would steady him, hold him, and keep him on track. He was right with God and at last Yates was committed.

Thirty-five

Joy started deep inside of Yates and bubbled up until it felt as if he could not hold it all. He left the altar and started the walk back to his seat thinking the glory of God must have shone on his face as he had seen it shine on Dollie's. Now he knew what Dollie meant when she said she felt light as a feather. That was exactly how he felt.

His sins were gone. Oh, the joy of salvation, of knowing he was back with God as the night, when just a boy, God visited him. Never again would he wonder where he would spend eternity. He knew beyond a shadow of a doubt that he would not end up in the pits of hell. Saved, sanctified, and filled with the precious Holy Ghost, he knew he was on his way to heaven. He had sweet peace and a blessed assurance.

Before he reached his pew, however, he suddenly felt a burden on his shoulders, a heaviness so real that he literally staggered under the weight. Bewildered, he cried within, *what is this, God?*

It took a few minutes before Yates realized what he felt: it was a sense of responsibility for a lost and dying world. Most of the people Yates knew were without God. They didn't even know about him, didn't know that Jesus loved them and died in their place, didn't know that He forgave sins, didn't know that He gave peace and joy.

Yates knew now that he was wrong about the Klan, wrong to believe that beating and killing people for their sins was justified. Only Jesus could change a person and He did it with love. Yates knew he had to tell everyone the good news about Jesus.

Thirty-six

The next morning in his favorite Ybor City Cuban Restaurant, Yates took his usual seat at the counter. The fire of the Holy Spirit burned within. He had to tell somebody.

"Something special happened to me last night," he said as the waiter poured Yates a steaming cup of coffee. "Things are different now."

"How?" the waiter said. "You look the same to me."

"I went to church and received the Baptism of the Holy Ghost."

"The what?"

"It's an experience," Yates said. "The Spirit of God comes on you and you speak in another language, one you've never learned, a heavenly language."

His waiter friend quickly wiped a coffee spill off the counter. "You speak this tongue?" he asked.

"I sure did."

"Speak it for me!" he shouted in his Cuban accent. All eyes in the place turned to the two men, all ears listening to this strange conversation. They waited for Yates' next words.

"I can't. The Holy Ghost is particular where He speaks." Suddenly a newfound boldness took over. Yates slid from his stool, turned and faced the restaurant full of people.

"God did a great thing for me last night," he said, surprised at the ease with which he spoke. "Like me, many of you come here every morning. You know me. You know the life I've lived, carousing in sin. You know that I drank and danced at the same nightclubs as you. Last night all that changed. I went to the altar at the Church of God on Buffalo Avenue to pray. I was so miserable because I wasn't sure where I stood with God. I had to know."

Then he began his story of how he met God on the highway, and how, the night before, he saw lights radiating from heaven and a dove descending. He told how God filled him with the Holy Ghost and called him to preach.

"I want to help you find this same God and the peace and joy I've found."

Yates looked around and saw that many eyes glistened with tears. Some patrons openly sobbed.

"You can receive God the same way I did. Get down on your knees and cry out to Him. Accept His Son Jesus who died for you. Tell Him you are sorry for your sins. He'll forgive you and save you just like He did me."

People got out of their chairs and knelt on the floor beside their table. They prayed with tears streaming down their faces, confessing their sins. Yates saw lives changed before his eyes. It was a glorious experience.

A few customers walked out laughing, but most of the people in the restaurant knelt to pray.

That day, Yates felt the joy that comes from helping another human being find God through his son Jesus Christ – a joy that nothing could take away.

Thirty-seven

All morning the joy Yates felt in that restaurant thrilled him. Excited about the people who knelt to pray, he thanked God for using him to lead others to Christ. But as the day wore on something else gnawed away at the happiness he had found. His peace and joy began to flicker and fade. There was something left undone – his promise to pay for the stolen squab. He knew he shouldn't put it off, yet he dreaded facing Mr. Pollock.

When lunchtime arrived, he headed the truck in the direction of Pollock's Fish Market, pulled into the parking lot and entered the building. The old fish odor greeted him. Suddenly he missed working with the man and woman who befriended him and became a second father and mother.

Mrs. Pollock stood behind the counter. She rushed around it and gave Yates a motherly hug. "Yates, I sure do miss that smile of yours around here."

"I miss you too, Mrs. Pollock."

"Can you stay for lunch?"

"No, I only got a minute, got to talk to Mr. Pollock about something."

"Maybe next time."

"Yes Ma'am." Yates smiled and turned to find her

husband, his hand a little shaky and his mouth dry.

Yates found him chatting with an employee and asked Mr. Pollock if he could speak to him in private.

Mr. Pollock slapped Yates on the back. "Good to see you, Kidd. Wha'cha need?"

This is not going to be easy. They walked to the side of the building away from the customers and Mrs. Pollock. Yates swallowed. "Mr. Pollock, a while back I came to visit and did something wrong."

"What? I can't imagine you doing wrong. Why you were one of my best workers ever."

"I wasn't as good as you think. That day before I left, I lifted two squabs from the meat case." He swallowed again and blinked knowing he had more to say. "Last night I found God. He changed my life and I've come to pay you for those two birds." Yates reached in his pocket, pulled out the money and held it out to him.

Mr. Pollock's eyes watered and he pushed Yates hand. "Put that money away."

"But I want to pay you, Mr. Pollock. I don't want anything on my conscience."

"Your coming here is pay enough." He grabbed Yates hand and shook it for a long time. "It took a real man to do that. I'm proud of you, Kidd."

"Please, Mr. Pollock, take the money. I promised God." Yates stuck the money in Mr. Pollock's shirt pocket.

Yates knew he had kept his end of the deal to pay his debt if God forgave him. Nothing stood between him and his God. He walked away with a smile on his face, a clear conscience and a spring in his step in spite of the limp.

Yates wonderful feeling of victory was not long lived. By the time he got back to work, the weight of worry over another situation settled down on him.

"Oh, God," he prayed, "I can't do that," . . . but he knew he had to.

Thirty-eight

As surely as the sun rose in the east and set in the west, that's how certain Yates was that he must leave the Klan. It would be hard. Few men left and lived to tell it. Through the years he thought he recognized two or three. It was strange to shake hands with a minister just introduced, feel the familiarity of the secret handshake and know that he was a Klansman in the past, too. There was a look in the eye of *knowing,* though neither man would speak of it.

Yates went to Folsom, the wizard of his area, to tell him he wanted out. His feet felt heavy as he slid from his truck, closing the door with a clang. The sun hid behind a cloud as he crossed the porch to the front door. His footsteps echoed in his ears and his heart beat wildly. The office was dark and the stale scent of tobacco smoke hung heavy in the air. Yates immediately felt nauseous. He was no coward, but the walls seemed to close in on him. He wanted to run.

Folsom sat at his desk and stood when he saw Yates, his chair scraping the wooden floor as he scooted it back. He stuck out his hand and seemed to sense the tension Yates felt. It showed on his face as he clenched his teeth.

"What is it Kidd?" He asked giving him the Klan handshake.

Yates mouth felt like it was filled with cotton. His voice sounded weak and hollow.

"I want out." All of the well-planned speech was gone, evaporated from his mind like the dew on a hot summer morning.

"Out of what?" Folsom frowned and spit out the words.

"I want out of the Klan," Yates said, barely above a whisper, beads of sweat broke out on his forehead.

Folsom's jaw tightened and he glared at Yates. "You're kidding, right?" he said through clenched teeth.

"I'm dead serious."

Folsom picked up a stogy and lit it blowing the smoke away from Yates.

"You'll be dead, all right."

All the color drained from Yates' face. "I can't stay in."

"Nonsense!" Folsom roared and hit the desk with his fist. "Why?' The word stabbed the air.

Did Yates dare tell him? He squared his shoulders and looked Folsom straight in the eyes.

"I'm different now," His voice was suddenly strong. Once started, the story gushed from his lips like the mighty Niagara – words poured out, one after the other.

"I found God, Folsom. I know it sounds crazy, but it's true. I found God. He made me into a new person. The things I was doing were weighing me down: all the drinking, smoking, beatings and killings. I just can't take part in 'em anymore. I've been convicted, but at the same time, forgiven."

Folsom stared at Yates like he thought he was off his rocker, but Yates kept talking faster and faster.

"God sent His son Jesus to die for our sins, and we all sin, Folsom, every one of us. I mean here we are punishing people for every little thing we think they do wrong, but then, we're sinners, too. It never felt right to me and now I know why. I've been saved, washed in the blood of Jesus and baptized with the Holy Ghost. I even spoke in tongues. And a peace washed over me like I've never felt before, you just can't even imagine it. The heavy weight of guilt I carried rolled off of me. I felt joy and love that I can't describe. God loves me, Folsom, me, a miserable sinner."

Yates stopped then, filled once again with the pure awe and wonder of it. He looked at Folsom, saw his jaw had relaxed and water gathered in his eyes.

"I just can't be a member of the Klan, not knowing what I know now."

Tears rolled down Folsom's face and dripped off his chin. "I envy you, Kidd" he whispered. "I'd give anything to be in your shoes."

"You can. You can do the same thing I did."

"No! It's too late for me. I'm in too deep."

"God loves you, Folsom. Accept him."

"I can't."

"Jesus died for you, too. He took your place on a cross. Believe in Him."

Folsom shook his head, his eyes dark. "I'd like to, Kidd, but I can't." He said it with a ring of finality. He added softly, "I'll do what I can to help you." He looked away then looked Kidd in the eyes. "I can't promise you nothing, though."

Yates nodded and thanked Folsom. It was over. He had done all that he could do. It was up to God now if he lived or died. Yates knew that his life was in God's hands, not this or any other mans'.

When he left the room Folsom followed. He used the back of his hands to wipe the tear drops still wet on his face. Both men emerged into the bright sunlight. The heavy load Yates carried into the building was gone. Feeling weightless he floated across the porch, down the steps and out to his truck. It seemed his feet barely touched the ground. Crawling into the cab of the truck, he felt a smile spread across his face, a smile he could not control.

He lifted his hand to Folsom, put the truck in gear, backed out, and headed home. His spirit soared. *I'm free. That's all behind me now.*

Still, for a long time, a little doubt now and then made him look over his shoulder.

Thirty-nine

Shortly after Yates sermon in the restaurant and his exit from the Klan, he had a vision. Alone in a room everything faded from his sight. In one corner of the room, a fountain appeared. People as far as his eyes could see gathered in a semi circle around the fountain. They were on their knees with heads bowed and shoulders bent beneath what appeared to be heavy burdens. In semidarkness they moaned because of their invisible loads.

The side of the room where Yates stood suddenly burst with light as an angel appeared. The tall angel, dressed in a white robe that glistened in the tremendous light radiating around him, took Yates by the arm. With his other hand he pointed toward the dry fountain and spoke.

"That fountain represents you. As water flows out of a fountain to give life to those who drink so spiritual water will flow from you to others, bringing hope. You will speak words of life. You will bless many."

Then Yates saw cool, clear, sparkling water cascade over the side of the fountain and flow out toward the people. They scooped up the water with their hands and eagerly drank. Refreshed and encouraged they lifted their heads and hands and praised God. The dark side of the room brightened into full light as the people radiated with joy.

As suddenly as he came, the angel vanished and the scene faded.

Yates was astounded at the beauty of the angel and the responsibility of the message. He felt the burden for lost souls the night he received the Holy Spirit, but now his eyes confirmed God's call on his life. Now he was certain that God wanted him to preach the Gospel of Jesus Christ.

Yates heart yearned to preach, but his mind knew if he answered the call to the pulpit, nothing in life would be the same and the differences might be too much for Dollie and Norma. He just couldn't put them through all those changes. Not yet.

Forty

For the next three years Yates and Dollie read their Bibles regularly and attended services at the church. They were eager to learn more about God.

Once a week the women of the church stood on street corners and handed out tracts, talked to people about their soul and invited them to come to church. While Yates worked, Dollie often joined the women. She stood for hours telling others what God had done for her.

Yates and Dollie were both amazed at how completely God had changed their lives. Still, they needed to grow spiritually. Later they would laugh when they remembered how God used the preacher to teach them a few painful lessons that started their maturity process.

One Sunday night Brother Roberts preached on telling lies. He said, "Yeah, you lie. You tell your children that there's a Santa when you know good and well there is no Santa Claus. You better repent of that lie before you die and go to a devil's hell."

Norma with her big blue eyes opened wide looked up at Dollie, shook her head and said, "There ain't no Santa Claus, Mama?" Tears spilled out of her eyes and rolled down her cheeks.

Dollie tried to comfort her with a hug. She decided

then and there that she would never tell another child about Santa. She wouldn't lie about being out of flour again, either.

The church believed in divine healing and spoke against using medicine or going to doctors, but when Norma developed a rash, Yates questioned the belief. He knew God healed and he wanted desperately to keep the rules of the church. He and Dollie prayed and prayed for the rash. Nothing happened. He hated watching Norma suffer and cry for relief.

Finally one day Yates read in the Bible, *Those who are well do not need a physician, but those who are sick,* (Luke 5:31). Yates believed that Jesus was saying it is okay to use doctors and medicine. He went into the drug store and bought a small tube of ointment the pharmacists recommended and rubbed it on Norma's leg. The rash cleared.

He decided that God created herbs used for medicine and God gave man the intelligence and knowledge to mix it. After that he trusted God, to a degree, for his own healing. However, if he prayed for his child and she were not healed right away, he took her to a doctor.

One night Brother Roberts paced back and forth across the front of the church exclaiming, "Listen to me. You put one of them devil inspired radios in your home and sit with your ear glued to it listening to all kinds of ungodly music and stories. You ought to be ashamed of yourself. God's not pleased. Throw that trash from hell out the window and read your Bible instead."

Yates promptly got rid of the radio at home and the one in his truck.

One Monday at noon a few weeks later, he rode by the parsonage during his lunch break to talk with Brother Roberts about a matter. On his way to the front door of the parsonage, he heard loud worldly music. He knocked several times. The pastor finally heard him and opened the door. Yates walked in. A radio sat right in the living room blaring away. Brother Roberts rushed over and turned it down.

"Brother Roberts," Yates said with alarm, "Why is a radio in your house? You told us to get rid of ours."

Brother Roberts grinned. "Aw, my boys wanted one and I thought I would try it out to see what everybody is listening to. It's not so bad."

"But you told us we'd go to hell if we listened to it."

"Well I say a lot of things. Can't pay attention to everything a man says."

Yates left in a daze. *I'll never go to church again and listen to a man who doesn't practice what he preaches.* All week he moped. He felt like a fool, duped by a man he trusted.

Saturday evening he saw his Bible on the coffee table. When he picked it up the pages opened to, *the heavens declare the glory of God; and the firmament sheweth His handiwork (Psalms 19:1).*

He caught his breath and relived the day he met God on the highway, the day he saw the picture of God's handiwork, the day the heavens declared God's glory to him. His eyes felt wet. He wiped them with his hand and read the verse again and again.

Flipping back through the Bible, the pages again fell open, this time he read, *the fool hath said in his heart, there is no God (Psalm 14:1)*. Suddenly Yates knew that he felt like a fool for nothing. He got rid of his radio because a man said he should. He was doing without his radio while the same man went out and bought one. That hurt Yates' pride. That's all there was to it. Pride wouldn't take him over again. Now he knew the only real fools are those who see the light of God's creation and in spite of its beauty, deny God's existence.

The next day when the church doors opened, Yates walked through them with a big smile on his face. He was no fool.

Later Yates found a scripture in Matthew 17:1-8. In this passage Jesus took three of his disciples up to a mountain where they saw Jesus transfigured. His face shone as the sun and His garment was white as the light. Moses and Elijah, who were dead, appeared and talked with him.

Impetuous Peter said, "Lord, let's build three tabernacles here, one for you, one for Moses and one for Elijah."

Before he finished his statement a bright cloud covered them. God spoke from the cloud and said, "This is my beloved son, in whom I am well pleased; hear ye Him."

When they looked up the cloud was gone and they saw no one but Jesus.

That day Yates made a decision. *From now on I'll keep my eyes on Jesus.*

Yates regained respect for Brother Roberts and

listened to him preach each week. He still admired him, and the two men built a strong friendship; however, Yates read the Bible for himself and made no decisions until he checked the scriptures to see what Jesus said.

He also checked the scriptures Pa referred to in the hospital, the verses about 'suing your brother.' After reading the words for himself, Yates better understood Pa's decision. It didn't make his limp any less troublesome and though he still didn't see it completely the way Pa did, a change began in Yates' attitude.

Forty-one

As it turned out, Yates and Dollie's salvation held unexpected benefits. Once Yates quit spending money on whiskey and cigarettes, they saved enough to buy a piece of land and began plans for their own house. Dollie was elated. For days she waved her hands excitedly as she talked about her new home.

They found three acres on the east end of Buffalo Avenue, out of the city, just past the bridge that crossed over Six Mile Creek. Yates saw his long-time dream coming to pass: there was enough room to raise chickens. He felt as excited about the place as Dollie.

Pa's building enterprise was booming. He had built a subdivision in Oak Park, made a fortune on it and promised to build Yates' and Dollie's house and even furnish some of the materials. After buying lumber and nails, he started construction.

Yates helped Pa in the evenings, after work and all day on Saturdays. He loved everything about building: the odor of the wood as he measured, sawed and nailed the boards in place; the feel of the sturdy wood in his hands. He loved being outdoors in the warm sunshine and he loved the feeling of accomplishment that made him smile and whistle as he worked. He even loved the tired feeling at night when he finally crawled between the sheets for rest. But the thing he loved most was the peace he felt as he worked side by side with Pa; Yates noticed that his old resentment toward Pa was gone.

He wasn't sure exactly when God helped him overcome it, but he remembered reading the Scripture, *Forgive us our trespasses as we forgive those who trespass against us (*Mark 11:26*).*

Yates had prayed that so many times and now he knew it had happened. He had forgiven his father and was glad to be rid of the hateful feelings.

They finished the three bedroom house, bought a few pieces of furniture: a new dining room set, a new chair for the living room and a bigger bed for Norma. The three moved in. Dollie looked around at all the extra room and had a sudden hankering to play the piano again, so Yates, always anxious to please his little wife, bought one. Dollie polished and waxed the piano until it gleamed, shined up the new furniture and decorated the house to perfection.

Yates and Dollie had begun to kneel around the table and pray before breakfast. It really helped get their day started right. Now, every morning when they knelt, they thanked God for the new house and all of His blessings.

One morning as they went down on their knees Dollie said, "Pray for me, Yates. I think I'm in the family way again. I don't feel so good."

He saw her face was paler than usual and noticed the greenish look around her mouth. Though he hated seeing Dollie sick he was happy with the possibility of another chance at the boy he longed for. He still felt tender when he thought about the one they lost. He knew God forgave him, but it was hard to forgive his-self. He pushed the thoughts to the back of his mind and instead thanked God, as the days went by, that Dollie hadn't miscarried again.

Dollie's appetite increased and her stomach soon was round as a ball. She didn't complain about being fat this time or mention dancing at all. The changes God had made were amazing.

This pregnancy went smoothly, except Dollie gained extra weight and carried the baby longer than expected. When she was two weeks overdue, she became concerned. Doctor Dyer encouraged her to walk more, but that didn't help. She took castor oil hoping to speed things up. Still nothing happened. Finally, a full month past her due date, Dollie cooked a big pork roast smothered in onions, baked an oven full of bright orange sweet potatoes and boiled a big pot of collard greens with bacon.

"This is the best meal," she said to Yates stuffing her-self. "I just can't get enough." She poured the juice from the cooked collards in a cup and drank it. "Umm, that pot liquor is delicious."

Later that night when the labor pains started she thought it was gas. She soon realized that it was more than the food.

Dollie wanted to stay home and have this baby at her new house. She sent Yates for the doctor. While he was out he went by to tell Mama Carter and picked up his teenaged sister Virgie to help with Norma. By the time he got back to Dollie her pain had increased.

"I don't think I can have this baby, Dr. Dyer," she

groaned as Yates walked into the room.

"Of course, you can, Dollie," he answered.

Dollie moaned and crossed her arms over her wide belly rocking back and forth she cried, "It hurts worse this time."

"I know, but you'll make it. This is a bigger baby than before."

"It's too big for me," she wailed.

When she saw Yates, her voice rose, "I'm dying, Yates. I can't stand this pain." Her eyes had the look of a wounded animal. Yates hated to see her suffer. He took her hand.

"You'll be okay, Dollie. God'll help you."

She turned her head away and gave a long guttural groan, sucking her breath back in through her teeth as the contraction increased.

When she was quiet again Yates slipped out of the room to check on Norma. Virgie was reading a book to her. As he opened the door another contraction started and Dollie screamed, "I can't stand this pain! I'm dying."

Norma's eyes grew wide. She ran and grabbed Yates around the legs. "Oh, Daddy, is Mama gonna die?"

"No, Honey." He patted her head, but she was not consoled. He bent down and took her in his arms. She laid her head on his shoulder and sobbed.

"Mama'll be all right. Don't worry, honey," his voice was soft and soothing. He held her close for a few minutes then pulled a sucker out of his pocket. "Look what I bought you when I went to get Aunt Virgie."

Norma looked at the candy, wiped her tears with the back of her hand and reached for the sucker. The next time he went to check on her between Dollie's contractions she had finished the sucker but was still upset.

"Daddy," she whimpered, "if the doctor brought the baby in his black bag like Aunt Virgie said, why is Mama crying like that?"

Yates picked her up again, but wondered how much to tell a four-year-old?

"This will all be over in a little while," he said. "Someday I'll explain it to you." He gave her another hug. "Mama will be okay." He set her down and went back to Dollie wondering if what he said was true: would Dollie be all right?

He thought of Dollie's small body and remembered Mama Carter's concern with the first baby. What would he do if something happened to his Doll? Maybe she was too small to have this baby and really was dying. *Oh God,* he prayed, *help my Doll.*

Back and forth Yates went from Dollie's heart wrenching screams to Norma's pitiful wailing and distressful questions. Deep inside Yates was thankful that he had made things right with God, yet he still fought worrisome thoughts that troubled him. He prayed with every step.

Finally about four o'clock in the morning Dollie gave one last gut wrenching groan with a tremendous push. Dr. Dyer announced, "It's a girl."

Yates breath caught in his throat as disappointment washed over him. He straightened his shoulders and reminded himself that the ordeal was finally over and his little tiny Doll was alive after giving birth to such a big baby, even if it was a girl.

Dr. Dyer laid the newborn in Dollie's arms. She examined the dimpled elbows and knees and the rolls of fat on the cherubs thighs. "My goodness, you look like you're already a month old," she cooed at the chubby baby.

"Well, Dollie, you did carry her for ten months," Dr. Dyer said and they all laughed. The humor was a welcome relief from the drama they'd just endured.

Yates was amazed at how fast a woman can forget the pain of childbirth. It was hard to believe that as soon as the infant appeared, Dollie was back to her normal, bubbly self though she did complain for years afterwards. When she sat too long, her hip hurt badly. She always blamed the pain on giving birth to a whopping ten pound girl.

They named the baby Barbara Ann, but almost immediately nicknamed her Bobbie. Yates still didn't have his boy, but knowing this baby girl had all of her parts, appeared healthy and Dollie was still alive brought him a lot of joy.

Norma felt displaced over the newcomer and wasn't happy at all. The only child for four years, she didn't want to share the limelight with this screaming little body who created such a stir and caused her mama so much pain. In spite of Virgie reading and talking to her during this frightening time, she was traumatized and wasn't about to accept her new sister.

When Dell and Paul heard the news they grabbed Tommy and came to visit the biggest baby ever born into the family. Upon arriving they saw Norma playing outside.

"Norma, what do you have in your house?" Dell asked in her vivacious way.

Norma put her hands on her hips. "A squall box and

you can have it!"

Stepping back Dell opened her mouth in shock, but soon recovered her composure. "Aw, come on, Norma, let's go inside and see your new baby sister"

"No!" Norma answered. "I'm never going in there!" She crossed her arms and sat on the steps, pouting dramatically.

The next day Yates bought Norma a horse swing and hung it from a limb on the big oak tree in the front yard. He helped her on and gave her a gentle push. The horse mane and tail swished in the wind.

"You know what?" Yates pulled the horse back and held it in the air.

Norma leaned on the horse's back holding tightly to the rope. "What?" she said.

He spoke softly in her ear. "You'll always be my firstborn little girl and hold a special spot in my heart." Yates kissed her gently on the cheek. "Nobody will ever take your place." He let go of the swing.

Norma turned her head and smiled at her daddy as the wind blew through her hair.

That evening Norma climbed on the bed beside Dollie and the baby. She lay on her stomach and for a long time stared at the infant. A smile broke across her face and she reached over and kissed one little arm. "Baby sister," she whispered then jumped off the bed and ran to find her daddy.

Forty-two

Yates whistled a happy tune as he stepped off the footage for the new chicken houses. Excitement built thinking about his new business. He visualized the long building completed and filled with white fluffy chickens laying their eggs.

"Great," he said under his breath. He raised and waved his right hand and cried, "Glory to God."

Yates changed jobs and now delivered animal feed for Allied Mills, which put him in daily contact with other chicken farmers. He read everything he found and became an expert on the subject, doling out advice when a customer had sick chickens. People began asking for his help. They called him the 'Chicken Doctor.' Yates was proud of his new title and thanked God for the opportunity to help others.

When Yates' own houses were filled, Dollie joined in the work and spent hours, many times until midnight, candling eggs. Sitting at a table she held the eggs, one at a time, in front of a glowing candle and later an electric light bulb. The light revealed the inside of the egg. Dollie knew if it was fertile or rotten. She separated them into baskets humming merrily as she worked. Really the noise was more of an "err," a sound she made when she cooked, cleaned the house, and did other chores that made her happy.

The sound of Dollie's hum made Yates happy.

Four-year-old Norma helped tend to baby Bobbie at Dollie's side. Norma constantly played too close to the eggs. Dollie warned her over and over. One day Dollie said, "Get away from the eggs, Norma before you fall and break them all."

Soon as the words were out of her mouth, Norma tripped and landed face down in the basket of eggs.

"See what happens when you don't listen," Dollie scolded. "Now, maybe you'll pay attention and mind."

Norma raised up and sobbed in horror as slimy goo ran down her face and tears mixed in with the slime. Dollie suppressed her laughter when she saw Norma's eyelashes stuck together. Through tight lips that kept tilting at the sides Dollie continued, "Bad things happen when children don't mind their parents."

Before long, she had cleaned Norma and the mess. She went back to work with Norma and Bobbie at a safer distance.

After that day, Yates occasionally took Norma with him on his delivery route while Bobbie took a nap. He thought Dollie deserved a break.

Nearly two years passed when one day Virgie came to watch the little ones while Dollie went to the doctor.

Dr. Dyer wrote on his chart as Dollie scooted off the examining table. He looked over his wire framed glasses. "This one's a boy, Dollie. I'm almost positive."

"Oh, I hope so. Mama thinks it's a boy too," she said, "but how can you tell?"

Dr. Dyer scratched his head. "Well, you are carrying it awfully low. I know It's an old wives tale, but I've noticed that women tend to have boys when that happens. Also the heart beat is faster like a boy's."

"That's great Dr. Dyer. Yates will be so pleased." She impulsively gave the old doctor a hug. "This is my last one. I don't think my body can take any more."

Dr. Dyer nodded. "I don't blame you, Dollie." He remembered her struggle with the last ten pound baby. "You've done your share of reproducing. Three's a-plenty."

She nodded and left to tell Yates the good news humming the Gospel song they sang at church, *Oh, I want to see him. Look upon his face.*

That evening at supper, Yates beamed when Dollie relayed the Doctor's words. "All right!" Yates short leg thumped as he got up and danced a little jig. "You hear that girls? You're going to have a brother." He stopped abruptly, took Dollie's hand while a big grin covered his face. "But you know, Dollie, I will love it even if it is another girl." He went to each daughter and kissed her on the head. "You know I wouldn't trade you girls for all the stinking boys in the world, don't you?"

Dollie rose from the table and he hugged her as tight as he could with her belly in the way then twirled her around.

"Oh, Yates, quit. That makes me dizzy." A big smile crept across her mouth. "Let's name him John Wayne." Her black eyes sparkled and she hurried to clear the supper dishes from the table.

"Fine with me." Yates caught her eye and winked.

"When we used to go to the movies, you always did like him," he teased.

A few weeks later Dollie awoke with the sun streaming in the bed room window. "Ohhh" she moaned rubbing the ache in her stomach. *Feels like my insides might fall out. Why did I eat all those sweet potatoes and collard greens last night?* Without opening her eyes, she ran her hand across the other side of the bed. Empty . . . Dollie sat upright, "Why isn't Yates here when I need him?" she said out loud. She heard the familiar sound of water on the chicken houses. "He didn't have to start cleaning those stupid chicken houses this early. He'll have to go for the doctor soon." She flung the bed covers back, "Yates!"

Before long old Dr. Dyer's Model T clambered into the yard. Yates returned with Virgie sitting prim and proper in the truck's cab. She wore a freshly starched and ironed cotton print dress. The doctor was opening his medical bag when they entered the room.

"Dollie, what can I do to help?" Virgie drew out her words and smiled sweetly showing her white even teeth.

"Tend to Norma and Bobbie," Dollie said curtly. She turned away and whined. "I'm really hurting, Dr. Dyer."

"You're having a boy, Dollie. Just keep your mind on that."

"I hope you're right cause I'm not going through this again for anybody. Ohhh, I can't stand this pain."

"Breathe through your mouth Dollie. Try to relax. It'll be over before long."

Dollie groaned and cried, "I can't have this baby.

It's too much work. It's killing me."

"I know it hurts," Mama Carter had arrived. "You can do it Dollie. Just keep thinking about that little boy you're giving Yates."

"Where is he?" Dollie was clearly put out with her husband. "You'd think he could clean those dumb ole chicken houses some other time. Ohhhhhhh!"

"Now Dollie," Mama Carter's tone was soft. "You know good and well that Yates has to tend to his work."

"I know he likes those chickens better than me or he would be in here with me. Ohhhhhh, I can't stand it Mama."

"You'll be all right," Mama Carter wiped Dollie's face with a damp cloth. "Try to relax. It'll soon be over."

"Who's dying in here?" Yates teased, coming into the room as sweat poured from his forehead and his shirt dripped water.

"Oh Yates, I need you here with me. Can't you tend to those ole chicken houses later? Ohhhhhhh! Yates the pain is killing me."

He bent over the bed and kissed her on the cheek. "I'm through with the work Dollie. I'll be here till this boy arrives." He grinned and winked.

"Oh Yates! You make me so mad sometimes."

"I know, Dollie." He pursed his lips.

"Don't kiss me again!" Dollie yelled.

Yates chuckled and turned to the doctor. "How can I help, doc?"

"Same as the last two times, Yates, stand there at Dollie's right knee. On the next contraction you push that knee and I'll push the left one."

After what seemed like an eternity of pushing, Dollie gave birth. Dr. Dyer's eyes were wide when he said, "It's a girl!" He shook his head and lowered his tone. "I was sure this one was a boy."

Yates felt crushed. He wouldn't ask Dollie to go through this again. His chance of having a boy was over. He had three girls and that was it.

Doctor Dyer laid the baby on Dollie's belly and Yates studied her face. He couldn't help but notice how much she looked like his wife. Suddenly he fell in love with the helpless infant. "She's beautiful. She looks just like you, Doll." He kissed Dollie again then turned back toward Doctor Dyer. "We'll keep her, doc."

"Oh, she *is* pretty," Dollie sighed. "She is certainly not going back where she came from even if she is a girl."

Mama Carter brought in a pan of warm water, laid out the tiny white, dress and took the baby. "What will you name her, Dollie?"

"Oh Mama, I don't know. I didn't pick out a girl's name." She turned to Yates. "What do you think?"

"It beats me." Yates shrugged and shook his head. "You women decide on that."

"Well, we certainly can't name her John Wayne," Dollie said stifling a sob. "Mama, help me"

"Use the name anyway. Call her Johnny." Mama Carter lathered the chubby baby.

"For a girl?"

"Change the spelling to J-o-n-n-i-e. That sounds like a girl's name."

"Yeah, it does."

Mama Carter looked at Virgie who came in to see

the newborn.

"Virgie, isn't your middle name Lee?"

Virgie nodded.

"Dollie, Virgie was so good to help you with the children you could name this baby after her: *Jonnie Lee*." Mama Carter laid the fresh sweet baby in Dollie's arms.

"That sounds pretty," Dollie turned to Virgie, "I'm so glad you came to help. That settles it I'm giving her your middle name."

Yates didn't have his boy but he had another beautiful nine pound girl with a boy's name, *Jonnie Lee,* one that was the spitting image of his Doll. He could live with that!

* * *

Dollie didn't understand why a woman had to lay in bed for 10 days after her baby was born. The longer she lay there the worse she felt. When at last the eleventh day arrived and her feet touched the floor she felt so weak she could hardly stand. It felt like her insides would surely fall out. She walked to the kitchen then collapsed in the nearest chair.

Yates stood at the sink looking out the window, a cup of coffee in one hand, a faraway look in his eye. He turned his head toward Dollie's sigh. "Morning Dollie," he smiled. "How ya feeling?"

"Tuckered out." she replied.

"Baby sleeping?"

"Yeah, Thank the Lord. I need to start my fruitcakes today."

"Can't you wait a day or two till you get your strength back?" Concern colored Yates' voice.

"No later than tomorrow or they won't have time to

get moist before Christmas. Umm. Wish I had a piece now."

Later that day Yates bought the necessary ingredients. Early the next morning Dollie rose, ate breakfast, nursed Jonnie and set about mixing flour, sugar, fragrant spices with candied fruit and nuts.

Baby Jonnie began to cry when she was barely started. She brought Norma's little red rocking chair into the kitchen.

"Norma," she called, "Come hold the baby for Mama."

Norma ran to her chair and sat rocking baby Jonnie while Dollie set about baking her cakes humming as she worked. Two-year-old Bobbie tottered around holding to Dollie's skirt-tail sucking her thumb.

Dollie baked enough fruitcake to give to Mama and Daddy Carter, Dell and Paul, Buddy and his wife Irma, Mama and Daddy Kidd, with plenty left over for Yates and Dollie.

"How's it coming, Dollie?" Yates smiled and said as he came into the kitchen for a drink of water.

"Oh, Yates, I've got enough cakes made for everybody!" Dollie was back to her exuberant self.

Yates' heart overflowed with gratitude to see the team work among his girls. *Life is good and God is on His throne. No harm could befall us.*

He headed back to his chicken houses. Before he walked out the door he turned back to look at his happy family snug and content in their own home. Just then a cloud hid the sun. How could he obey God and do what he knew he had to do?

Forty-three

All night, two months later, six-year-old Norma struggled for air. Yates and Dollie feared she would die in the night from this latest asthma attack. Before bedtime Dollie suggested they turn a ladder-back kitchen chair upside down on the sofa for Norma to lean against making it easier for her to breathe. Yates fixed the chair, but still it looked as if every gasp for breath would be Norma's last.

Two-year-old Bobbie slept contentedly in her crib and the new baby Jonnie cried occasionally when it was time to nurse. Between times Yates and Dollie struggled in prayer. They tried to believe that God heard them, but no answer came. When the sun finally announced a new day and Norma seemed no better Dollie said "Yates, let's pray one more time before you go to work."

Yates agreed and they prayed again, but nothing happened.

In desperation Dollie turned to him and said, "Yates, when are you going to obey God?"

He felt her words hit him hard. They jarred him to his soul.

She waited for an answer.

"What do you mean, Dollie?"

"You know what I mean. When are you going to

obey God and *preach*?"

His mouth dropped open. *How does she know? I never told her that I am called to preach!* Three years had passed since Yates saw the vision. It was time to make a decision.

"I'm going to do it, Dollie! I'm going to preach the gospel!"

"Daddy, I can breathe!" Norma jumped up from the sofa knocking the chair over in her haste. "Mama, look." She took a deep breath and let it out through her nose. "I can breathe." Tears welled up in her eyes.

She ran to Dollie who hugged her and said over and over, "Thank you, Jesus, thank you, Jesus."

As soon as she let Norma go, Yates grabbed her and twirled her around laughing and going up and down on his short leg.

"Glory to God!" he shouted.

Norma's breathing problems ended when asthma left on the wings of Yates' promise to preach the Gospel of Jesus Christ. Yates realized Dollie knew about his call to preach because the same Spirit that called him lived in her, too, the Holy Spirit.

He had made the promise. There was no turning back.

Forty-four

Something was wrong. Bright red blood filled the toilet bowl every time Yates urinated. He didn't want to worry Dollie and tried to hide it, but she noticed anyway. They prayed and asked the church to pray, though they didn't reveal the problem. Nothing changed and Yates grew weak. Finally, in desperation he went to the doctor.

After tests, the doctor called Yates into his office with the results.

"Have a seat Kidd. We need to talk."

"What's wrong with me, Doc?"

"You have a kidney ailment called Bright's disease."

"What's the cure?"

The doctor slowly shook his head. "At the present, there's no cure."

Yates staggered and grabbed the table next to him before taking a seat. "How long?" he mumbled.

"No one really knows. With a dietary change you may see some improvement, though I know of none that have been what I would call successful. He looked down and whispered, "You may live six months or you could hemorrhage to death at any moment. I'm sorry, Kidd." Grabbing his pad and pen, he scratched out two prescriptions and handed them to Yates. "I suggest you take these, quit your job and set your house in order."

Yates stumbled out of the doctor's office and somehow made the trip home. Death loomed ahead like a thief. *So this is how a condemned man feels - a man on death row.* At home, he tossed the prescriptions on the dining table.

"Aren't you going to get these filled?" Dollie asked when he delivered the news.

"No. What's the use?" He shook his head. "I'm going to trust God. Either He'll heal me or I'll go on to heaven."

"Yates! You can't leave us!" Dollie sobbed.

He put his arms around her and drew her close. "I'm going to fast and pray for three days and wait on God."

Yates decided to work as long as he had strength. He didn't see any reason to quit work if he was going to die anyway. Day after dreary day he went on sheer willpower, forcing himself to work in spite of his swelling hands and feet and the pain in his back. He dragged through each day and collapsed the minute he walked in the door. He and Dollie continued to pray.

"Yates, I feel like the door to heaven has turned to brass and our prayers bounce back and hit us in the face," Dollie said one evening after prayer.

Yates nodded. "Me, too."

In the following days Yates grew weaker until he could barely get out of bed, but he would not give in.

One evening on his way home from work, tired and discouraged, he passed the spot where he met God on the highway three years earlier. Memories ran through his mind like a movie. He visualized himself throwing away the whiskey bottle and his deliverance that followed. He thought about the night he knelt at the altar and received the Holy Spirit with the assurance that he was right with God. His commitment to be true echoed in his ears. He remembered the vision and the call on his life. Finally he thought of the day Norma was healed of asthma after he promised God he would preach the gospel.

I don't understand it, God. Why did you call me to your work if I am going to die now?

In the distance, Yates heard a train. Up ahead, the railroad crossing lights flashed a red warning to stop. Gates slammed down across the track. He applied the brakes. The truck screeched to a halt. Yates looked down and there on the seat beside him sat his Bible. It replaced the whiskey bottle that made its home there before his conversion.

The air outside the truck was oppressively hot and not a tree or bush stirred. As the train whizzed by, a strong gust of wind blew through the truck window opening the pages of his Bible. They rustled and turned. Yates grabbed the open Bible. Words leaped off the page.

Dost thou believe on the Son of God? (John 9: 35).

He looked up through the windshield to the sky. "Yes, Lord, I do believe on you." He shook his head and continued, "Lord, the doctor said I could die anytime." He took a deep breath. "You are God and you healed my Daddy of tuberculosis and my daughter of asthma. I know you can heal me." Something caught in his throat as his eyes misted. "If you don't see fit to heal me, I'll be seeing you in a few days. Either way is fine with me, Lord. It's up to you."

Suddenly, Yates felt something warm touch the top of his head. It traveled through his body and came out the ends of his fingers and toes. Sitting right there at the railroad crossing Yates knew he would live to preach God's word.

The next time he went to the bathroom there was no sign of blood.

Forty-five

After Yates' healing, he knew he could no longer put off preaching, but he was troubled over what he thought God wanted him to do first. Every time he opened the Bible. Scripture after scripture leapt from the pages.

√   The kingdom of Heaven is like treasure hid in a field . . . A man . . . goes and *sells all that he has,* and buys that field, (Matthew 13:44.)

√   When he had found one pearl of great price, (he) went and *sold all that he had,* and bought it, (Matthew 13:46.)

√   Jesus said unto him, if thou wilt be perfect, go and *sell all that thou hast,*
      (Matthew 19:21.)

Yates slammed his Bible closed. *Lord, are you really asking me to sell my house?* He struggled with the question for days. *I can't do that to Dollie.*

He opened the Bible again. This time he read about how Abraham took his wife, Sari from the security of his father's house. They wandered going where God led. He took care of them and made them rich. Yates wasn't worried about being rich he only wanted to provide for Dollie and his girls.

Yates thought of Dollie's love for her home. She'd always had a secure place to live. *What right do I have to sell the house and expect her to follow me, only God knows where? I promised her daddy that I would provide for her. What about our three children? Aren't I responsible for them? I have to furnish food and a place to live, don't I?* Back and forth he tossed the questions.

He felt the house as a weight around his neck. It choked him and tied him to a public job. But he was afraid to untie it, let it go and trust God to come through for him. He wasn't sure he had that kind of courage. This walk of faith scared him.

His decision came after days of struggle when he read, *Whosoever he be of you that forsake not all that he hath, he cannot be my disciple,* (Luke 14:33).

The next day he put the house on the real estate market. He believed he had to go all the way, or nothing, so he told the agent that the furniture went with the house, including Dollie's beloved piano and also his long dreamed of chicken houses.

In three days everything sold.

Yates had already spoken to the State Overseer about assigning him to a church. Jake Roberts was a member of the State Council and recommended him. Within days, Dollie discovered a letter in the mailbox.

"What's this, Yates?" Dollie waved the letter toward him her eyes dancing.

"Read it Dollie." he swallowed.

Dollie tore open the letter and read, "You are appointed as pastor of the Church of God at Lake Thonotosassa. God bless you in your work."

A smile covered Yates face, a grin so big it felt like it might crack. "We have a church and place to live." He grabbed Dollie into his arms.

"And it's not too far away." She nestled on his chest. "We can still visit with our families."

Yates heart beat rapidly on moving day. Excitement coursed through his veins. He had helped Dollie pack their clothes, dishes, pots and pans and linens, the few things Yates believed it was okay to keep.

Dollie had a hard time fighting back tears that were just below the surface when she left her home. When she saw the parsonage all the light left her eyes and her lips were drawn in a straight line.

The tiny house had never seen a drop of paint. Ugly grayish/brown weathered boards were visible inside and out. Much smaller than their own house it was one room with a sofa and two double beds, plus a kitchenette with a half table that seated two.

"Is this it, Yates?" Dollie's voice quivered.

Yates nodded. "Afraid so."

"Where will we eat?"

Yates looked out the back door. A wooden picnic table sat under a big oak tree.

"Look, Dollie, we can have a picnic."

She looked out and nodded. When lunch time came she made sandwiches and sweet iced tea. "Dinner's ready, Yates. Come on girls, let's go outside and eat."

Norma and Bobbie grabbed their dolls and headed for the door giggling.

"A picnic!" Norma said.

"Picnic." Bobbie copied.

Jonnie lay sleeping on a pallet. "I'll nurse her when we come back in," Dollie said to Yates. She grabbed a couple of bananas to add to their lunch and he took out the pitcher of tea and the glasses.

The family joined hands and prayed over the food. Yates kept his hand over Dollie's. "We'll fix this place up, Dollie," he said. "I know it's not very big, but we can paint and make it look better." He whispered, "Soon as we can afford the paint."

"Okay," Dollie's lips quivered as she passed out the sandwiches.

Unless it rained, they ate outside on the picnic table every day. A cool breeze made it more pleasant than sitting in the stuffy little house. In rainy weather they took turns sitting at the small table that seated two. Thankful to have a roof over their head, they knew God had not failed them.

* * *

One Saturday, a few days after moving into the parsonage, Yates took Dollie by their former house for one last look. Dollie gasped when she saw all of her former furniture sitting out in the yard. Tears ran down her face at the sight of the piano she loved out in the weather.

"What if it rains, Yates? My piano will be ruined." She looked so sad, it tore at Yates heart.

"Don't worry, Dollie," he said, "God will give you another one in His time."

"I hope so." She sat silent and stared out the

vehicle window. In a few moments she wiped her eyes and turned to Yates, "It's okay." A smile lit her face, she took Yates hand. "I would rather you preach, than own the whole world."

Frustration that tormented Yates melted away. With Dollie in agreement nothing was impossible. Together they could trust God for everything.

* * *

As soon as the house was in order Yates began his pastoral duties. First he checked the books and found the membership roll then asked Dollie to go with him to meet their members.

He knocked on the first door.

Dollie put a little spit on the tail of Jonnie's gown and wiped a speck of dirt from Bobbies face. She turned to Norma and said, "Now Norma, you and Bobbie sit down when we get inside and don't touch anything." She nervously pushed Norma's hair behind one ear. "You girls are the preacher's daughters. You have to be good."

The door swung open. A lady with questioning eyes stood in the opening.

"Good morning, Sister Smith," Yates said with a smile. "I'm your new pastor, Yates Kidd. This is my wife, Dollie, and our girls: Norma, Bobbie and Jonnie." He extended his hand.

Sister Smith shook his hand. "Glad to meet you." She nodded at Dollie. "Come on in Brother and Sister Kidd." She stepped aside as they entered. "Have a seat."

"Thank you," Yates said.

Dollie sat on the sofa holding Jonnie. "Girls sit right here beside me," she said to Norma and Bobbie, "and remember," she whispered, "Don't touch anything. You might break it."

"Oh, don't worry about them. They'll be fine," Sister Smith said with a smile. "You folks must have wanted boys, with those names, Bobbie and Jonnie."

Dollie smiled back and said, "Yes, we thought for sure the last one would be a boy. Even the doctor thought so, but we love our girls."

"I wouldn't trade them for all the stinking ole boys in the world." Yates said laughing.

Sister Smith chuckled. "Boys are harder to raise, at least mine were. They both broke my heart when they got married and quit going to church."

"That's too bad," Yates said. "Tell me where they live and I'll be glad to give them a visit and invite them back to church."

"You would do that? Oh, thank you, Brother Kidd." Joy shone in her eyes.

After a few minutes of conversation, Yates said, "Can we pray with you before we leave?"

"Oh, yes. That would be so nice. It's been a long time since a preacher prayed in our home."

Dollie laid Jonnie on the couch while she, Norma and Bobbie got down on their knees. Yates knelt at his chair and Sister Smith at hers.

After prayer when they all stood, Yates said, "We'll be going now. We just wanted to get acquainted and let you know we're here to help in any way we can. Let us know if you ever need us. We'll be right here."

Water glistened in Sister Smith's eyes. "Thank you. Brother Kidd."

"We expect to see you Sunday for our first service," he said.

"Wouldn't miss it for anything." she said. "I want you folks to eat dinner with us after church Sunday."

"That would be real nice," Yates said.

Dollie swallowed hard and tried to smile. Her eyes roamed around the room and stopped at the kitchen. It seemed tidy and clean. At least they could eat inside. "Thank you for the invitation, it was very kind of you." She gave a half smile as they left.

One morning, after days of visiting members, Dollie gathered the breakfast dishes from the picnic table and started in the house, "Yates, I need a break today. Do you mind if the girls and I stay home?"

"What's wrong/" Yates cleared the rest of the table and followed her into the house.

"We've been so busy I haven't had time to wash clothes."

"Okay, Dollie. I'll fill the tubs for you before I go."

"Thanks."

"Yates started out the door to the pump. He turned back, "Dollie, we were going to visit that widow. It won't look good if I go alone."

"Skip her today and I'll go with you tomorrow."

After Yates and Dollie got acquainted with all of their members, Yates visited businessmen and workers in the community inviting them to church and praying with anyone who would let him. The work never ended.

At the end of the first month, the church clerk

handed Yates the portion of tithe money for the pastor. He lowered his head. "I'm sorry it's not more, Brother Kidd."

Yates eyes widened when he looked down and saw his salary for the month - one dollar and fifty cents. He swallowed around a lump in his throat and wondered how he would feed his wife and three children. The money saved from his job was nearly gone. Then he remembered the scripture about God feeding the birds and how Jesus said that people are of more value than birds.

Yates voice quivered when he said, "Don't you worry, Brother." He smiled and added, "God will meet our needs."

The State Overseer took note of Yates' work and rode out to visit. "You sure are doing a good job here, Brother Kidd," he said. "I'm proud of your church's growth."

Yates nodded. "Before long we'll need a bigger building. I've been jotting down plans on paper."

"Is that a fact? Well, since you're such a go-getter, I had an idea I'd like you to try."

"What is it, Brother?"

"I'd like you to go over to St. Petersburg, run a revival, and start a new church there. It's close enough that you could drive back and forth and still look after your own sheep here." The overseer looked over his glasses and grinned. "There are a lot of service men in the area. We need to reach them."

"I'll do anything you feel led of the Lord for me to do." Yates agreed, laughing. "If you believe my church won't suffer, I can start next week."

For the next few days a feeling of dread hung over

Yates.

"What is it, Lord." he prayed. "Did I miss your will in agreeing to go to St. Petersburg?"

Dollie didn't tell Yates, but she felt a heavy burden, too. Something was wrong. She didn't know what, so she got down on her knees beside the bed and cried out to God for help in whatever lay ahead.

Yates arranged to have the meeting in a storefront and advertised in the newspaper.

People came. Yates preached about the love of God, giving his testimony of how God delivered him from alcohol, cigarettes and a life of sin and shame. God's power moved in each service and the anointing flowed like a river. The homemade altar filled every night with people hungry for God, crying out to Him for salvation.

The uneasy feeling stayed.

"Lord, I'm trusting You," Yates prayed.

In bed one night after the wonderful manifestation of God's power and witnessing souls born into the kingdom, an evil voice from the past whispered in his ear, *You're a fool, Kidd. Selling your home and putting your wife and children in that little cracker box of a house. Something bad is about to happen to you. Your wife and children won't even have a place to live. God can't take care of you. He won't. What about your leg? He didn't take care of that. You're still a cripple, limping up and down while you preach. Some example you are.*

Yates covered his ears and whispered, "I trust you, Lord. I will be true, I will be true."

Dollie stirred from her sleep. "What's the matter, Yates?"

"Got an uneasy feeling," he said.

"Its okay, Yates, you can go to sleep. I've already prayed and God's got His hand on you."

The revival advertisement caught the attention of the wrong people. One night when Yates had long forgotten about the Klan . . .

Forty-six

The black, 1938 Ford sedan sped along the dark street. Slowing, the driver cut his car lights as he approached the storefront. Cars lined the street around the building. Light streamed through plate glass windows across the structure's front and revealed a room full of people. Inside naked light bulbs hung from black cords in the ceiling and glared. A man with one hand in the air stood in front of the crowd on a temporary platform made from discarded flats; a man they called Kidd.

"Whew! Look at that crowd." Spotting an empty space across the road the driver silently eased his car in, parking near an old oak. Both doors sprang open when the vehicle stopped. Two sets of well-shod feet touched the car's running board before descending to the sandy soil. The man on the passenger side brushed a strand of Spanish moss from his face. He snatched it from the tree, tossed it aside and exited the car. With the same motion, he adjusted his felt hat a bit more over one eye.

Meanwhile, another man, a stranger to the two in the black car, had arrived a moment earlier and stood in the shadow beside his car. Duty at the Navy base kept him longer than he expected. Late for the meeting, he came anyway, eager to hear Kidd speak.

He felt his crisp, white hat to make sure it sat properly and flicked a piece of lint from his navy bell-bottoms. He adjusted the square back collar of his shirt and touched the knot of his sailor tie to see that it lay in the right spot. After rubbing a little dust from his spit shined shoes, he stood tall and straightened his shoulders.

He had taken one-step toward the building when the red glow from the brake lights on the darkened sedan faded and it pulled into the empty spot. He watched as the doors opened and the unidentified men jumped out of the automobile. He heard the low growl of their voices.

"This won't take long." With a tight jaw, the man from the sedan faced his driver. He stuck his hand in the lower front pocket of his pinstriped jacket and lifted something out.

The sailor stepped back in the shadows and watched as an eerie glimmer of light from the street lamp flashed on a gun barrel. The man from the dark sedan opened the pistol and twirled the cylinder to check for bullets. Satisfied he closed the gun and waved it toward the building.

"I'll open the door and cut him down while he's preaching," the triggerman snarled through clenched teeth.

The driver nodded. He walked to the back of the car and leaned against the trunk to get a good view of the action, ready to jump in when it was over to make a fast getaway.

"I don't know who Kidd thinks he is," the driver sneered. "He oughta know he can't get away with insulting the Klan." He spit on the ground. "Hurry up and bump him off and let's get out of here."

Grasping their mission, the sailor held his breath

and waited for their next move. He stood stiff, glued to the ground. He watched wide eyed, listened, and wondered, *who are these men? Why do they want to kill Kidd?*

The man with the gun strode to the door, his head high like a rooster about to attack. When he got to the door, he grabbed the knob, but he didn't go in. Instead he quickly jumped backwards with a howl of pain. Moaning he grabbed his arm and hightailed it back to the car crying, "Let's get out of here! I can't move my hand, it's paralyzed!"

His partner jumped away from the car. "I didn't see nothing. What happened?" He ran around to the passenger side and opened the door for the gunman.

"When I touched the doorknob, electricity or something went through my hand."

The two men leaped into the car with the gunman shouting, "Get me to the hospital!"

The sailor stood with mouth open as the car sped away its tail lights disappearing into the darkness. The next moment, he darted from his place in the shadows and burst into the building interrupting Kidd's message, His voice rose and fell as he tried to tell him what had just happened.

"T-t-two men were out there." He pointed to the door. "I s-s-s-saw everything." He tried to get his breath.

Yates stopped in mid sentence. "What are you talking about, Hank?"

Hank could hardly speak. He took a deep breath. "Two men . . . out there . . . one of em had a g-g-gun." He let out a long breath. "Came to kill you!"

In unison the congregation gasped.

"Where are these men?" Yates felt no fear or dread,

only eagerness to face them believing a host of angels surrounded him.

"Gone." The sailor's voice quivered. "When the man touched the door knob, his hand froze or something. He said something about electricity hit him and his hand was paralyzed. They took off for the hospital."

"Let me check that door knob." Yates started toward the door.

"No!" The sailor shouted. "Let me."

He rushed to the spot, grabbed the knob and opened the door. With his other hand he took the outside knob and turned it. He let it go, grabbed it again and again.

"Nothing's wrong with it."

Two men close by took turns checking it. Nothing.

Hank looked at Yates, his eyes wide. "Brother Kidd, God just spared your life."

The congregation jumped to their feet and praised God to the top of their voices, waving their hands in the air. Some took out handkerchiefs and waved them while others danced a jig.

Yates looked at Dollie standing at the front bench with sleeping baby Jonnie grasped tightly in her arms. Norma and Bobbie lay on the bench, sound asleep. He thought about the consequences had the man reached him. His beautiful Doll and sweet daughters would be without a husband and father right now. When he could not see the danger, God did.

I will be true. The words echoed once again in his ears, the words he promised God at the altar. He knew this time it was not his words to God but God's words to him.

God was true.

Yates raised one hand, waved it side to side and shouted, "Well, Glory!"

Tears trickled down Dollie's cheeks. She raised one hand, holding Jonnie with the other, closed her eyes and said, "Thank you, Jesus, thank you, Jesus, thank you, Jesus." The simple words came from the bottom of her heart. She was truly thankful that her husband was alive. God was faithful.

Yates hurried to the front row patted sleeping Norma and Bobbie on the head, drew Dollie and the baby into his arms. He held her close and whispered in her ear. "For the rest of our lives Dollie, we don't ever have to wonder or be afraid. God is big enough to take care of us."

Dollie looked up at him, her brown eyes sparkling with tears. "I know, Yates." She nodded and smiled through her tears. "I know."

Yates hugged her again and whispered, "I love you, little Doll."

She whispered against his shoulder, "I love you, too, Yates."

He turned back to his makeshift pulpit in the storefront building and gave his appeal." If you want to know a God big enough to take care of you, come and kneel at this altar. He is a God who loves you so much that He sent His son Jesus to die in your place, so that you can escape the dreadful fires of hell and go to a wonderful place called heaven, a place where the streets are paved with gold and you live forever and ever in a beautiful mansion. All he wants is that you accept his son, Jesus, forsake your sins and love God with all of your heart." He finished his appeal with one word, "Come."

The front of the church filled.

Hank was the first one there.

Yates never heard from the Ku Klux Klan again. Several times, through the years, he extended his hand to an unknown man who met it with the familiar secret shake and Yates wondered if they had sent this man to finish their mission, but he was not afraid.

He trusted the God who healed his father of Tuberculosis, the God who forgave him and Dollie of their sins, the God who delivered him from alcohol and nicotine, the God who healed him of Bright's disease and finally the God who protected him from the Klan's hit- man. He knew this God could do anything.

He believed without a shadow of a doubt the words in *Matthew 19:26, with God, all things are possible.* But, through the years, his faith was tested again and again.

Acknowledgements

Cassie Selleck - Thank you for taking time to critique my writing week after week. I learned so much from the hours spent with you in our writers group.

Marietta Skeens - Your friendship and opinions of my work are highly valued. We had good times going to our jail ministry every Tuesday with you reading my words and helping make them better as I drove the car.

Vernelyn Haggarty - Your care and prayers for this book encouraged me so many times. Thank you for being my friend, reading, correcting, and urging me on.

Bernice Talent - Your interest in helping get this book published will not be forgotten.

Dennie Jo Jones - Thank you for using your secretary skills in grammar and punctuation.

Amanda Dansby - Granddaughter, I won't forget how you helped me by letting me read my entire book to you (in little bits of course). You offered so much help with your wise suggestions and teen age perspective. The way you said, "Oh, Granny, that's so good," thrilled my heart.

John Whittington and Jason Taylor – Thanks for your computer expertise. Thank you Jason for creating the cover.

Thanks to all other friends who read the unpublished work

and encouraged me to continue.

Uncle Roby – thanks for much of "Bee Hunting" and the story on the train.

Malcolm Whittington -Thanks loving husband for putting up with me over fifty years.

Thanks to the Lord Jesus Christ who makes us able to do all things. I felt this book had to be written, Mama and Daddy's story told.

About the Author

Jonnie Kidd Whittington, born at Six Mile Creek in Tampa, Florida, is the daughter of Yates and Dollie Kidd. Married to retired minister, Malcolm Whittington for 56 years, Jonnie played piano or organ and taught Bible classes in his churches. A mother to three, grandmother to eight and great grandmother to one, she continues to teach piano at Lighthouse Christian Center and Academy, where her youngest son, John is pastor. She also writes and teaches Bible Studies for local churches, one being where her son-in-law, Dale Dansby is pastor. He is married to her daughter, Deborah.

Look for Jonnie's next book - Kidd's Daughter, Another Spitfire – the continuation of Kidd and Dollie's life from her view point as a child. She desires to tell you what Kidd taught her about life and eternity.

Jonnie would love to hear from you. Write to :jonnienotes@gmail.com or http://www.jonniewhittington.blogspot.com/ for her blog.

Made in the USA
Charleston, SC
20 February 2014